OVER COFFEE

Julie Surface Johnson

Over Coffee

We Shared Our Secrets

A Novel

WinePress Publishing (PO Box 428, Enumclaw, WA 98022) functions only as book publisher. As such, the ultimate design, content, editorial accuracy, and views expressed or implied in this work are those of the author.

ISBN 13: 978-1-57921-973-4
ISBN 10: 1-57921-973-X
Library of Congress Catalog Card Number: 2008930443

To my husband, Dick,
and mother, Glennice Surface (1923–2007),
who encouraged me to write, despite all odds.

To God,
who wouldn't let me keep silent.

"Open your mouth for the speechless,
in the cause of all who are appointed to die."
—Prov. 31:8 (NKJV)

May our Lord Jesus Christ himself and God our Father, who loved us and by his grace gave us eternal encouragement and good hope, encourage your hearts and strengthen you in every good deed and word.

—2 Thess. 2:16–17

CONTENTS

Acknowledgments xi

Chapter One: Getting Acquainted 1
Chapter Two: Releasing Balloons 15
Chapter Three: Carly's Confession 21
Chapter Four: Annie's Trip to Haight-Ashbury 53
Chapter Five: Emma's Transformation 71
Chapter Six: Susan's Route to Respectability 101
Chapter Seven: A Trip to Seattle 125
Chapter Eight: Mariah's Search for Acceptance 135
Chapter Nine: Liz's Lost Boy 157
Chapter Ten: Continuing Friendships 179

Coffee Shop Favorites 183

Over Coffee Group Discussion Questions 187

Carly's Resource List 201

Guidelines for Small Study Support Groups 205

About the Author 207

Acknowledgments

Warmest gratitude to my family for their love and support.

Special thanks to Cheryl Baxter, Anne Paden, Connie Bless, Stefanie and Mike Hodder, Stan Baldwin, Jim Byrne, Kim Davidson, and Pat Roberts for their friendship, insight, and critiquing skills.

Sincere appreciation to those who labor selflessly in pregnancy resource centers around the world, saving lives and mending hearts.

Chapter One

Getting Acquainted

Call me Liz—Liz the barista. For the uninitiated, that's a person trained in the art of making espresso coffee drinks. I own and operate Over Coffee—not one of those famous franchises, but rather a homey little storefront on Broadway Street in northeast Portland, Oregon.

It took me some time to find my true calling; but, at age forty-nine, after my last chick flew the coop, this little red hen decided to try her wings. I can't fly very high, of course, but I do love brewing a good, hot cup of coffee and serving it to an appreciative customer. People come and go—my favorites are the regulars who seem to need me as much as my coffee.

When asked for advice, I can be strong like a French Roast, somewhere in the middle, like a good Colombian, or mild as Costa Rican. I read people. I can tell when someone is suffering by a downcast eye, a toss of the head, a far-off look, or a droop of the shoulders. Body language. That's all it is.

As a woman who raised two daughters, I'm particularly tuned in to the body language of women. Many suffering women come into my coffee shop.

Yesterday, for example, business was slow . . . one middle-aged man sat at the bar sipping an espresso. Then a young mother came in with her two small girls and ordered a latte for herself and steamers for her children. I was working on their orders when I heard a commotion.

"Don't look at my daughters like that."

"What are you talking about?" The man's face registered shock.

"I saw the way you looked at them. Ever since we came in, you've been gawking. They're just little girls. Keep your eyes to yourself, or I'll report you to the authorities."

"Lady, you've got a problem," the man growled, and he stormed out the door.

I glanced from him to the young mother and, glimpsing fear in her eyes, guessed that she had suffered abuse in her past, probably as a little girl, perhaps the age of her daughters.

Such things happen. Over the months I've drawn many women into conversation and they've revealed things to me—their joys, their sorrows. Many of them suffered injustices, such as child abuse, rape, and abandonment, with all the related consequences. Others mentioned a problem I wasn't familiar with—"post-abortion stress." One day, when talking with a friend who works at a nearby pregnancy center, I asked if she knew anything about it. Did she ever!

"Of course, I know about post-abortion stress," said Annie. "I see women almost every day who are suffering from it. *I* suffered from it."

How could this be? I've known Annie for years and consider her one of my best friends. Why hasn't she told me about this? What were the circumstances?

"What do you mean you suffered from it?" I asked. "Why haven't you told me about this before? You had an abortion? When?"

"It was long before we met." Annie shrugged her shoulders. "It's ancient history. Did you say you have some customers with PAS?"

"With . . . what?" I asked.

"You know, post-abortion stress. What we're talking about."

"Oh, sorry," I said. "I didn't catch the acronym. Yes, several of my customers have mentioned it. But what exactly is it?" Obviously it had something to do with the aftereffects of abortion; but other than that, I was clueless.

Annie swished her cappuccino with a stir stick, mixing in the foam. "It means different things to different people, and some suffer more than others. For many women, there's depression, sorrow, feelings of guilt and shame. Some, like me, have difficulty relating to men and children. Many suffer from 'anniversary reactions' on the anniversary of the abortion or the aborted baby's expected due date. Personally, I don't think I could have survived without assistance from a recovery group."

"How come you never told me about all of this, Annie? Maybe I could have helped."

"Have you had an abortion?"

"No," I said flatly.

"Then you probably couldn't have helped me."

"Well, maybe I could have. At least, I could have tried."

"Bless you for wanting to help," Annie said with her characteristic smile. "Someday I'll tell you what happened, but not today because I'm already late for work."

"In the meantime, how can I help my customers?" I asked.

"There's a post-abortion recovery group connected with the pregnancy center. The leader's name is Carly. If you like, I could talk to her about starting a group for your friends."

"Sure, that'd be great," I said as Annie gathered up her things and headed for the door. "Thanks."

"I'll call you after I've talked to Carly." Annie walked briskly away, closing the door behind her.

My head was spinning. Annie had experienced something so painful she couldn't get over it without help from a support group—and she'd never told me, her close friend, about it. What was going on here? Just how serious was PAS? And were my customers currently in as much pain as Annie once was?

Then I began to wonder. *Do I want to get quite that involved in the lives of my customers? Probably not. But they're more than customers. And I owe it to them to at least make an effort. Annie said she couldn't have survived without help.*

• • • • •

A few days later, Annie called. "I've spoken with Carly and she is free on Wednesday nights if you'd like to get a group together."

With Annie's help, I made up a flyer that described upcoming meetings of H.E.A.R.T., an acronym for Healing Encouragement for Abortion-Related Trauma, and gave out copies selectively. Within a week and a half we had our group: Annie; her friend Carly; my customers Emma, Susan, and Mariah; and myself. Annie and Carly knew all about PAS and had found healing, while Emma, Susan, and Mariah were currently suffering with PAS. I, on the other hand, knew virtually nothing about it at all. *But,* I thought, *when has that ever stopped me from jumping in where angels fear to tread?*

Carly came to see me and explained that because I was not post-abortive, I'd need to bring to the group another issue I was struggling with. That wouldn't be hard. I knew exactly what I would bring. *Abortion isn't the only painful issue women face,* I thought.

My coffee shop, Over Coffee, would become our meeting place. Perfect. People are used to serious discussions here. These walls have heard everything. By closing early, I could host the group from eight to ten o'clock on Wednesday nights. It would be a welcoming refuge, a safe place. I would see to that.

• • • • •

When the day of our first meeting arrived, I wasn't sure how to prepare. I wanted Over Coffee to be the kind of place where women felt safe talking about difficult issues. But what exactly does that look like? I experimented some and finally settled on a cozy arrangement of three bistro tables in a circle.

Close to arrival time, I put on pots of regular and decaf Colombian and, humming to myself, I carefully studied the room—café curtains drawn against the night, table lamps lit, coffee smells permeating the air. *Very welcoming. Yes, heavy hearts will be lightened here. Lives will be changed.* Little did I know how much they'd be changed or how desperately needed those changes were—not just for the three struggling with PAS, but for all of us.

Then I began to have second thoughts. What if the shop wasn't conducive to our meetings? Maybe it wasn't a formal enough setting for serious discussion. What if there were too many distractions outside on Broadway Street or the sirens from the nearby firehouse were too noisy?

As it turned out, that was the least of my worries. Five stick figures arrived: everyone seemed awkward, uncharacteristically timid, embarrassed. What was going on? I hadn't seen this side of Susan or Mariah, and particularly not Emma. My desire had been for this to be a good experience, but I began to wonder if I had made a huge mistake.

Looking around the room, I smiled at these women who had originally seemed eager to participate in such a group. There was thoroughly postmodern Emma Matthews, twenty-two years old, single, college-educated, tech job. She loved caramel lattes "with skim milk and extra caramel, please." Emma, the world traveler . . . looked like a little girl alone in a foreign land without passport or friends. She smiled back timidly and then quickly glanced at her feet.

Emma, where's your "glad to know you" smile, your flashing brown eyes, your youthful enthusiasm?

Next was Susan Garrett, forty-five years old, divorced, single mother of two teenagers, bookkeeper. Tall and attractive, poised and confident, her preference was decaf vanilla latte. Susan returned my smile but I saw her lips quiver.

Susan, I thought I knew you. Quivering lips? You've gone to the mat for your children in situations where I'd have cowered in fear. Where's your spark?

Mariah Martin, thirty-two years old, factory worker, abusive boyfriend, lived with her mother. Painfully shy and withdrawn, black-rimmed glasses. Mariah had few friends. For some reason, she liked hanging around Over Coffee and usually ordered coffee-of-the-day, decaf, with room for cream. Mariah didn't return my smile; rather she looked heavenward as if praying for help or deliverance.

Mariah, it will be all right. Don't be afraid. This is supposed to be a good thing. If not, heads will roll!

Annie Johnson, fifty-five years old, widow, no children, comedienne. Director of a pregnancy center, she was used to talking about abortion with frightened young women; her easy, breezy style helped them face their options. Annie had a taste for cappuccino with lots of foam, over which she sprinkled way too much nutmeg.

Carly Collins, our fearless facilitator, twenty-nine years old, married, two girls, church secretary, not one of my regular customers—yet. Very pretty with soft black hair and copper-flecked brown eyes, she radiated confidence.

And then there was me, Liz Smith, nearing sixty, husband Bill, two married daughters, three grandsons. I was responsible for ensuring that everyone in this group felt safe: at the moment, things didn't look too good.

I gave Carly a look that said, *do something!*

She nodded as if to say, "Chill, Liz. You may be twice my age, but I can handle this." And she did. With her calm manner and ready laugh, she soon convinced us there was nothing to fear.

"I'll bet some of you are wondering what you are doing here," Carly said. "You may be asking, 'How did I get drawn into this? Whose big idea was this anyway?'"

"Yeah, Liz," Annie quipped, looking at me. Everyone laughed. I blushed.

"Well, not to worry. This will be a safe place. We are not here to judge one another—or to rescue one another. We are here to work out some emotions that have been festering for a long time, things like anger, denial, bitterness, depression. It won't be easy, but it will be good. When we're finished with our work in twelve weeks, you should all experience freedom and a better understanding of yourself and others."

And so commenced our Bible study support group. We began by discussing the character of God—we learned that he is approachable, he loves us, and he will forgive any sin we have ever committed.

Talking about God's forgiveness seemed to help because by the time we were getting up to leave, everyone seemed more comfortable. However, that's when we got the news that the following week we'd be briefly sharing our personal stories with one another. That meant they'd all be talking about their abortions and I'd be talking about the day I became an unfit mother.

• • • • •

I waited till morning to pick up after our meeting. With the sun streaming in through the café curtains, I couldn't help but contrast the mood of last night's session with the dawn of a new day. *Will this group be helpful to my customers? Or am I just putting them through an exercise in futility? This post-abortion stress thing—is it real or just an attempt to label unexplainable feelings some women have?*

Rearranging tables and washing them, sweeping the floor—I felt that, along with the sun, a new day was dawning for me. Don't ask me why. I didn't even have post-abortion stress. Yet when Carly stated, emphatically, that God's forgiveness reached to any sin, I clung to the hope that it reached to mine.

When everything was arranged and in its place, I flipped the closed sign over and unlocked the front door.

Within ten minutes, Susan came by the shop for her usual decaf vanilla latte. *No one has a right to look so put together this early in the morning. I wish I were tall.*

"You could have just spent the night," I teased, motioning her to sit down. "What did you think of the H.E.A.R.T. group last night?"

Susan pursed her lips, raised her right eyebrow and said, "I'm thinking of dropping out. I can't imagine talking about my abortion for ten minutes—especially not to a group of strangers."

My heart sank. *Is Susan going to be the first of my customers to feel I've let them down?* Smiling, I said, "Susan, I don't want you to do anything you don't want to do. But I keep hearing how effective support groups are in dealing with all kinds of problems. I'd like to see you give this a try. And, anyway, who says it has to be ten minutes?"

Susan looked at me curiously. "Isn't that what Carly said?"

"So what if she did. If you can tell your story in five minutes, go for it. Just come. Sit by me. I'll hold your hand if it'll make you feel better."

She made a face. "Good grief. I'm not a baby. No, I'll come—but do sit across from me so I can look at you when I tell it." She climbed on a barstool. "Now, where's my latte?"

• • • • •

The next day Emma came by on her lunch hour. Adjusting herself on the same barstool Susan had used, she said, "I'm not sure what to think about the support group. Nobody talks much. How can we support one another if nobody talks?"

That's what I love about Emma and her generation. They tell it like they see it. "I'm guessing that will change as we all get more comfortable with one another. At least I hope so. Talking about our problems can be a good thing; and it's been my experience that women usually understand one another."

"I suppose so," Emma said, impatiently. "I guess we'll see on Wednesday."

Good. At least Emma is planning on giving H.E.A.R.T. another try.

Mariah didn't stop by at *all*; I worried that she wouldn't be back. Shy beyond belief, Mariah is a puzzler. You can't help but wonder what's going on in her head . . . as well as in her life.

Annie dashed in for her cappuccino but dashed back out again when she saw three people ahead of her in line. "Catch you later, Liz."

The days passed slowly. Sunday morning my husband, Bill, and I went to church as usual. Sitting in our customary spot, second row from the back on the right, I paid particular attention to the cross hanging on the wall. Empty. Jesus died, rose again, and paid the price for all my sins. *He loves me; he forgives me. But why, oh why, can't I forgive myself?* Bill handed me his handkerchief—I hadn't realized I was crying.

• • • • •

When Wednesday finally rolled around again, I organized the tables into a circle and wondered who else had had a hard week. Looking outside, I noticed that it was raining cats and dogs. *Will anyone use this as an excuse to stay home?* It was, after all, the night we were to share our stories.

To my relief, everybody came. With a lightened heart, I greeted them with hugs. "I'm so glad to see you all. Come, take off your coats and warm up with some coffee. Tonight we're having French Roast—regular or decaf. And I have a plate of biscotti to pass."

Carly slipped out of her wet coat and surveyed the group. "I'm glad to see you, too. And proud of you! You didn't let a little rain stop you from coming to this important session when we tell our stories."

"Believe me," Emma said, "I thought about not coming. But then I remembered Liz saying something about women understanding one another, and thought I'd see for myself." Wrapping her hands around the coffee cup, she shivered.

Should I turn up the heat . . . or is she shivering from nervousness?

"I came for the biscotti," Annie said, and everyone laughed. Ever the comic, my dear friend Annie was always good for easing tension in a room.

One by one we told our stories, as much as you can tell of life-transforming events in ten or fifteen minutes. And one by one we let down our guard, allowing others inside. It wasn't as hard as we had feared because we soon learned a tremendous lesson—everybody makes mistakes.

We cried together, the tissue box circling time and again. Little pats, teary smiles, understanding nods. We identified with one another, empathized with one another. We were a group—better than a group—we were confidantes.

Susan told us how she felt when her uncle Bob raped her repeatedly and threatened to harm her and her parents if she ever told anyone. When she became pregnant, he took her secretly to an abortion clinic. She shared her shame when he lied about her age and implied that she had been "fooling around and this was the end result of that." The memory was so painful for Susan that she hadn't been able to deal with it all of these years. But in finally telling it to others, she felt a small sense of release.

With us to protect her, young Emma remembered the day she saw her baby on the ultrasound screen and chose to abort it anyway. She wept at her callousness, recalling that she had said, "I'm just not ready to have a baby now. It's not a good time for me."

Mariah, sweet shy Mariah, remembered the day she was gang-raped by some neighbor boys. A young teen, she'd been afraid to tell anyone until finally her bulging stomach gave her away. Her mother had dragged her to the abortion clinic, yelling at her all the way. Mariah remembered how her mother had told the abortionist to just "get it done." Though Mariah didn't want the abortion, she was too frightened to tell anyone. She was too frightened to save her baby's life. "How can I live with that?" she asked.

Annie had been a flower child in San Francisco in the sixties. She had "made love, not war" and conceived a child during her "hippy" year. Her experience with abortion had scarred her for life, emotionally as well as physically.

Carly had been a "good little Christian girl," so good that she fantasized over what it would be like to do something risky, something out of character, something bad. And so she had become involved with a young man who definitely was not a "good little Christian boy." Next thing she knew, she was pregnant. Realizing she had fallen into a hole she herself had dug, Carly decided to take the "easy way out" and secretly obtained an abortion. Having turned her back on all she had once held sacred, Carly became deeply depressed and suicidal. It took years before she found healing in a support group similar to ours.

Listening to these women talk, I couldn't help but notice how multi-faceted their stories were. There are many pathways to sorrow, and these women could just as easily have been attending a support group for child abuse, rape, youthful indiscretions, immature thinking—you name it. But abortion was the issue that had brought them together and it was because of their abortions that they were seeking help.

As the only woman in the group who was not post-abortive, I nevertheless felt a kinship with them all. Why? Because though I'd carried my child to term, I had turned my back on him—as surely as any of them had done to their babies. My son Jeremy died after eight days of life, died in the arms of a nurse because his mother was not able to face his deformities. His mother had fled the scene, abandoning her child to the care of strangers. His mother was unfit. I proved it in that act of betrayal.

Like the rest, I faced my demons in the company of friends. We cried together, dreamed together, even laughed together for comic relief. And in the end we were still standing . . . bruised but not broken.

Telling our stories was just the beginning. Over the weeks, Carly walked us through the difficult issues of denial, anger, depression, bitterness, and forgiveness. Because we had repressed many of our painful memories, dragging them up again was hard work and emotionally exhausting. Yet Carly explained it was a necessary part of healing—and we trusted her.

Each of us, some more successfully than others, learned to look at our situations through adult eyes, through a filter of grace. We learned to accept the guilt that was ours and also to divest ourselves of guilt that was not ours.

We came to understand that in confessing our guilt, we acknowledged our need for God's forgiveness, and, in accepting it, we began to experience the Great Physician's healing powers.

The next step was to extend forgiveness to those who had a part in our poor choices. We learned that we would only experience freedom from pain when we could walk away from the past and follow Christ into the future.

By the end of the eleventh week, all but one of us could say we felt better about ourselves.

Chapter Two

Releasing Balloons

We'd been promised something special for Week Twelve—something about balloons. And so it was that Carly gave us each our choice of colors and asked us to write messages on them, personal messages of repentance, forgiveness, blessings . . . whatever. Then our small band of balloon-carrying women left the coffee shop and walked to a nearby vacant lot.

Balloons in hand, we each prayed quietly over them and released them to the heavens.

Transfixed by the sight of balloons spiriting off in all directions, I heard muffled sobs from women releasing far more than their balloons. All too soon, nothing remained but a vast expanse of darkening blue sky. We were alone again, alone with our thoughts.

Our eyes met. Grasping hands, we hugged silently and headed back to the coffee shop where I placed steaming pots of coffee on the counter. With swollen eyes and sniffling noses, they helped themselves and walked silently to the tables.

"Would anyone care to share your feelings?" Carly asked, her voice seeming to echo against the café walls.

The subsequent silence made my skin crawl, the hairs on my arms standing straight up. My thoughts raced. *Maybe it's cold in here. I'd better turn the heat up.* But before I could move, Carly cleared her throat.

Unruffled, she looked around the tables at us and said, "Releasing the balloons has this effect on almost everyone. On the one hand, it can be hard to let go of painful memories because they've become such an integral part of who we are. On the other hand, releasing the balloons symbolizes freedom—freedom we experience when we learn to accept God's forgiveness for poor choices we've made. Only then can we extend forgiveness to ourselves and, finally, to others. It's like being forgiven and set free . . . to live again."

I looked around the tables at these women who had shared their most intimate feelings over the past twelve weeks. What was it I saw in their faces? Were these tears of sorrow or of joy? Who would speak first?

And then the dam burst. Everyone started speaking at once.

Carly laughed. "Wonderful. Let's take it one at a time."

"Carly." I looked toward the voice. It was beautiful Susan, eye makeup streaking her cheeks. "When I released my balloon, I felt this surge of emotions that I haven't been able to sort out yet. There's joy, and there's even some pain in there. But one thing I feel strongly—releasing my balloon was like releasing Uncle Bob's grip. The little girl is free at last, free to live and move on with her life."

"Me, too!" said Emma. "I feel free . . . and relieved because releasing my balloon means I'm willing to forgive myself for my selfishness, willing to let go of negative self-talk." Thrusting her fist in the air, she said, "Yesssss!"

Annie explained she had dealt with all these emotions in her prior recovery group. However, this time when she released her balloon, she reminded herself to *continually* release feelings of guilt and shame. "When God forgives a sin, it's forgiven. I don't need to hang on to it and beat myself over the head with it."

Mariah was overcome with emotion and could scarcely speak. However, she did say that with her balloon she was freeing herself to begin to live. When Carly asked her what she meant, Mariah mumbled something about her mother and then fell silent.

Carly said that her balloon was a gift she was sending to her baby, now living in heaven.

I listened to all their comments with puzzlement. I didn't feel the release they all felt. I didn't feel forgiven and set free. I'd wanted the balloon to symbolize my son—flying heavenward, free to live with his Creator rather than here in the guilty conscience of his unfit mother. But, like a pit in the bottom of my stomach, he was still here. I sensed his presence.

Like Mariah, I mumbled something unintelligible and fell silent.

Finally, Carly looked at the clock. "It's late. And, I'm sorry to say it, Liz, but these chairs are only comfortable for two hours."

Annie sighed, a smile spreading across her face. "This has been such a sweet time, I wish we didn't have to break it up yet."

"Do we have to? My apartment is nearby," said Emma. "We could go there." Emma's eagerness to keep the group together blessed my heart. What I had hoped for in the beginning had actually happened—the H.E.A.R.T. group had helped my customers begin to find inner peace.

"I'm with Emma," I said. "I feel like we know a little bit about one another, just enough to make me want to know more. What do you say we spend some time really getting to know one another?"

Her eyes narrowing, Mariah looked at me. "What do you mean by 'getting to know one another'?"

"Just sharing about our lives, what makes us tick. It seems we're on the fast track to friendship and I, for one, want to see where that leads." I looked at the others for feedback. "What do the rest of you think?"

"At least come see where I live," Emma said. "Then, if you ever want to, you can stop in. I'm always looking to make, and keep, good friends."

With that, the six of us packed up our belongings and moved to Emma's place—a gathering of former strangers who had grown to trust one another with our deepest secrets.

• • • • •

If forced to guess who lived in this apartment, I'd have chosen Emma hands down. On entering, we were drawn into a bit of Tuscany—ochre and brown walls, tan sofas and burnt-orange pillows. Fat sage-colored candles, set randomly on old mirrors, decorated the mantle and tables.

Offering us a choice of mineral water, chai tea, or white wine, Emma placed bowls of chips and salsa on the table. With a flick of a switch, she lit the natural gas fireplace. We were good to go.

But go where? What was the next step?

Again Carly, the veteran, took the lead. "I've got an idea," she said. "Liz suggested we share more about our lives. I'm comfortable doing that since I speak publicly all the time. Let me start by simply expanding on what I've already told you about myself."

Selecting a place on the sectional where she could see everyone, Carly sat down, pulling her legs under her. She smiled, then spoke.

"Twelve weeks ago we were strangers. Yet here we are, in many ways as close as friends, even sisters, because we've shared our lives with one another. We've been transparent and have let one another enter our worlds. In the process, we've learned that we share many common experiences that crippled us for years. In talking about these things, we've found, or are finding, wholeness again.

"So as I tell you the unabridged version of my story, please hear it for what it is—my story. This is what happened to me; and I am living with the consequences."

Chapter Three

Carly's Confession

I grew up in the Pacific Northwest, an area that prides itself in social consciousness. We're big on environmentalism and things like the snail darter, spotted owl, and Greenpeace.

As a teenager, however, I wasn't much interested in social concerns. I just liked having a good time with my friends, playing soccer, going out on group dates. Life was good. My folks were great; and I had a handsome big brother who had lots of attractive friends. Our home was the place to go for a fun time—guaranteed.

Sometimes it worked to my disadvantage that my brother and I were close. None of his good-looking friends dared even to look at me or else they'd have to deal with Kurt. Nobody was going to mess with Kurt's little sister.

Or could it be something else? I worried that I wasn't pretty enough and began to have one of those typical teenage complexes. I thought I must be too fat, my nose too big, my eyes set too far apart. Nobody could convince me that these things weren't true. If I were so beautiful, where were the dates? Why was no one asking me out?

• • • • •

Emma fidgeted. Annie snickered. I noticed the women in our group eyeing one another. Finally, Emma voiced what we were all thinking. "Carly, if you looked anything then like you do now, you'd *know* it was Kurt chasing them off. Haven't you looked in the mirror lately? You're gorgeous!"

Carly blushed, her head dropping, black curls falling forward. *That's so much a part of her charm. She's beautiful and doesn't even realize it.*

Carly cleared her throat, smiled, and continued her story. . .

• • • • •

Finally, I caught the attention of a boy. All right, he was a young man but, looking back, he had the accumulated wisdom of a twelve-year-old. I was with friends in the park when Eric Endsmire rode by on his motorcycle. He was cute . . . and did I mention he was riding a motorcycle?

I don't know why that was so important to me, except that I'd always been a good little girl, playing it safe. I was seventeen and still hadn't kissed a boy—really kissed, I mean. Eric seemed daring, a little edgy, and I was ready to take a risk.

At first, it was enough to sit behind Eric on the motorcycle, wind blowing through my hair, arms wrapped around his waist, flying down the freeway. Straining to hear what he said over the chopper noise, I finally gave up and let my mind wander into territory I'd never entered before. I'm ashamed to admit that this good little Christian girl had all sorts of wickedly sensual ideas.

It was exciting to me that Eric was able to do what he wanted when he wanted. No one checking up on him, he lived alone. Though he was underage, somehow he was able to purchase liquor and bragged about his supply of "booze" in the cupboard of his apartment.

• • • • •

That got another rise out of Emma. "Carly, Carly, don't you snooze. You've gotta watch out for the guys with booze!" We laughed, all but Susan.

"Sorry," she said. "Having a daughter that age, I don't think it's so funny."

"You're right," Emma said. "I'm sorry for interrupting. Please, Carly, go on."

• • • • •

I wouldn't go to his apartment. Maybe I was afraid of him or of what we might do there. So we'd just ride around town, stop at parks, window shop, go for a soft drink. There wasn't much to talk about; we had nothing in common. I was from a happy, caring family; Eric had been kicked out of the house when he was sixteen. I loved school and soccer, Eric had flunked out of school and had never participated in sports. I had lots of friends, Eric seemed to have none.

The first time Eric kissed me, I wasn't sure I liked it. *What was that smell? Cigarettes?* Yet, it was exciting. He had taken me in his arms, and pressed me to himself . . . hard.

When Eric released me, I felt weak and wasn't sure what to do. It was a kiss, but when I looked in his eyes, they seemed vacant . . . like he wasn't there. Even as young and inexperienced as I was, this didn't seem right. I asked him to take me home and told myself that if he ever called again, I would not be available. He was just too scary.

But when Eric called the next day, my resolve weakened, and I agreed to meet him at the park—just to talk. Sitting on a bench, I told him I didn't feel comfortable with him, that his kiss had confused me, and I didn't understand why he lived all alone. Where was his family?

After some prodding, Eric opened up and told me about his past. His dad had left when Eric and his brothers were all under age five. His mother had tried to raise the boys by herself and had done the best she could, but she had given up somewhere in Eric's early teen years.

She then allowed a succession of men into their lives to help pay the bills. Most of them were down-and-outers who contributed little and took the only thing she had left, her self-respect. As the oldest son, Eric tried to defend her against the unwanted advances of the men, but his mom's last boyfriend, Charlie, beat him up so badly he nearly had to be hospitalized.

Eric said his mother blamed him for all the trouble and ordered him out of the house. She said that she and Charlie would get along just fine with Eric gone. She called Eric "cunning" and said she knew he'd survive on his own.

Eric was devastated by her words. Furthermore, at age sixteen he had no money and no place to go. Fearful of the streets, he claimed to be eighteen so he could stay in rescue missions and worked whenever and wherever he could. In time, he found employment with a landscaping crew and made enough to pay expenses. He knew he could earn more if he moved to California but wanted to stay nearby to keep an eye on his mother and brothers. I saw that as a noble trait in Eric.

He admitted to having feelings of jealousy for the life I lived. He wished he had a family and friends and a real home. But this was not, as he said, "in the cards" for him.

Well, as you can guess, though my better judgment said to run the other way, my heart went out to him. I wanted to make his life better, to share some of my blessings with him. However well-intentioned I was, the end result was not what I had planned.

Feelings of pity, I guess, caused me to let down my guard. When Eric needed to swing by his apartment, I agreed to go up, just for a minute, so I could see where he lived.

I was shocked: it was so bare . . . a card table, two folding chairs, an old black and white television set, a bed, clock radio, a box for his clothes. Basically, that was all he owned. Yet, what he owned was clean and orderly.

I was ashamed when I thought of my room at home. So much stuff! And I took it all for granted! Half the time I couldn't find what I needed because it was hiding under so much clutter.

Why did I have so much and Eric had so little? In my childlike mind, I wanted to make up for all the injustice in his world. I wanted to hold him and tell him everything would be all right, that I would share my things with him.

How can I blame Eric for misinterpreting my feelings for him? When he saw my tears and the way I looked so tenderly at him, he reached out to me and held me close. Soon his lips found mine and in a frenzy of love and tears mixed with pity and sadness, I shared with him the most precious gift that I owned.

• • • • •

Carly glanced around the room at us. What was she looking for—our disapproval, shock? We all sat spellbound, then Emma spoke for all of us. "Don't stop now, Carly!"

Carly sighed . . . and continued.

• • • • •

I can't say this is when I got pregnant because Eric and I continued to have sex whenever possible. It wasn't love; it was pure lust. However noble my intentions started out, I was soon using Eric just as he was using me, to bolster a flagging ego, to prove to myself that someone found me attractive.

Over the months my family and friends noticed changes in me. They tried to help but weren't sure what the problem was. I know Mom suspected something, but I was so discreet it was difficult to pin me down. I was living a double life. For the most part, I entered into all my old activities, including my church youth group, but I saw Eric on the side whenever I could.

Finally, the inevitable happened. I skipped a period. This threw me into a tailspin. My cover was blown. Now everyone would know that I wasn't the good, fun-loving girl that others admired. What would my brother, Kurt, think? What would his friends think? What would my friends think? And Mom? And Dad—oh, no, Dad! His little princess had fallen off her pedestal.

I thought about marriage—to Eric. That would have been the "honorable" thing to do. But I didn't want to marry Eric; and I was sure he wouldn't want to marry me. No! I wouldn't go there. I had wanted to make his world better, not make mine worse.

It seemed I had only two options: carry the baby or abort it. If I carried the baby to term, I had options—I could either parent it or relinquish it for adoption. But the bottom line was that people would know. On the other hand, if I aborted the baby, no one would know, and I could go on with my life—only this time without Eric! Definitely without Eric!

It wasn't hard to decide . . . I'd abort. I wouldn't even tell Eric—why muddy the waters any more than they were? What if he tried to get me to keep the baby? What if he wanted to marry me after all? How would I get rid of him? No. I wouldn't tell him.

When Eric called that night, I asked Mom to say I wasn't home. That was a big mistake—asking her to lie for me. She guessed something was wrong, but I threw her off the trail by telling her I was trying to break up with him. Was that a sigh of relief I heard? Mom hurried back to the phone and told Eric I wasn't at home. When she returned to my bedroom, I pretended to be asleep.

Early the next morning, Eric came to my house. He said he needed to talk with me about something important. Deciding to take advantage of this opportunity to break up with him, I got on the back of his motorcycle. He headed straight for his apartment (no more meetings in the park for us). Walking inside, he began to unbutton his shirt and head for the bed. I sat on one of the two folding chairs.

"What did you want to talk about?" I asked.

"We can talk later. Let's make love first." Eric laughed, apparently tickled with himself.

Angry at Eric's deception, and even angrier that I was carrying his child, I yelled at him. "Make love? You don't love me. And I don't love you. It's time we broke up, Eric."

A look I can't describe crossed Eric's face. Was it pain? Shock? Sorrow? I don't know, but it wasn't what I'd expected. Then tears and sobs—heart-wrenching sobs—shook his body. *What have I done? Dear God, please make him stop.*

But he didn't stop. Eric didn't seem to notice or care that I was in the room. It was as if the dam had broken on his stored-up pain, and it was all coming out.

I didn't know whether to leave or stay, to lay a hand on his shoulder or keep my hands to myself. Hadn't I got myself into all this trouble out of pity for him in the first place? *Be strong. Be strong.*

Finally, Eric wiped his eyes and blew his nose. He looked at me as if seeing me for the first time, as if I were a total stranger.

"Carly, I don't get it. I thought you knew I loved you. It didn't dawn on me that you didn't love me. I thought we were a couple and that we'd get married someday, settle down, and have children. I knew I couldn't ask you till I had something to offer." He searched my eyes. "You do love me, don't you, Carly? I–I just couldn't take it if you turned me away. First my mother . . . now you."

Eric began to groan. "You love me, don't you, Carly? Don't you love me, Carly?" Rocking side to side, he repeated it over and over and over again.

Forgetting my own problems, I realized that Eric was in trouble and needed help. But where to turn? I thought of his mother but didn't know how to contact her. I thought of 9-1-1. Was this what they would call an emergency?

"Eric, I'm going to call 9-1-1 and get us some help. Okay?"

"No, Mom. I only need you. I need you, Mom. Please, don't make me leave. I don't know where to go or what to do. Make Charlie go, not me. I'll get a job. I'll work for us. Please, please . . . ."

Yes, by anyone's definition, this was an emergency. I dialed 9-1-1. They came for Eric, and they took him away. And I confess to you with great embarrassment and shame that I never saw him again.

• • • • •

Carly looked at our little group and fell suddenly silent. Her mouth was partly open and her eyes were partly closed. Furrows lined her forehead and tears began to stream from the corners of her eyes. As Carly collapsed in tears, we all rushed to console her.

This was a part of her story we hadn't heard, and I realized once again how complex the issues are . . . how deep the scars left by unwise decisions and careless choices.

After several minutes, Carly regained control and asked us to help her find out what happened to Eric and to do whatever was possible to make things right with him. None of us knew just what that would look like, but we agreed to walk through it with her.

After several minutes, Carly continued her story.

• • • • •

That night, I called my best friend, Kelly, told her my problem, and asked her to help me. She agreed, and the very next morning, she went with me to Planned Parenthood. I have to tell you right up front that they lied to me. They said that abortion is less painful than childbirth and that I would be able to go on with my life. Well, I have since found out that neither of those statements was true.

I don't need to tell you about the abortion process—all of you, except Liz, have your own set of memories. And besides, I just can't go there again. Let's just say it was a nightmare; my baby died, but I had to go on living . . . without raising suspicion.

Blaming menstrual cramps for my lack of energy bought some time but I knew I had to resume my normal activities. I tried to hang out with my old friends, to participate in the youth group. But I felt like such a phony! Good little Christian girl covering up her ugly abortion.

Surely those around me could sense my fear, see the guilt written all over my face, a scarlet "M" painted on my forehead proclaiming to all that a Murderer sat in their midst.

I believed that if anyone found out about my abortion, I'd be an outcast for sure. In my teenaged mind, I saw Christians as lovers of babies and, therefore, haters of women who aborted them.

Of course, now I realize that isn't true. If there's one quality that describes a true Christian, it's humility. Jesus taught that the right to cast the first stone is reserved for him who has not sinned. No true Christian would say he has not sinned! I realize that now—but I didn't then.

Over time, I began to back away from involvement of any kind. It was an act of self-preservation, but it came across as rejection to people I held dear. Confused, they began to shun me.

Only Kelly knew about the abortion. Yet even she couldn't begin to understand how I felt. How could she? No one who hasn't been there can understand the feelings of guilt and shame, the uneasiness whenever the topic of babies comes up. No one can understand the grief surrounding Mother's Day celebrations and the knowledge that one little baby will never celebrate his mother. Nor can anyone understand the wrenching panic that accompanies the sound of a vacuum cleaner—no, not unless they've been there.

For the first time in my life, I preferred to be alone or at home with family. Mom, Dad, and Kurt . . . they were my lifelines to a safer port.

Kurt said to me one day, "Carly, I'm worried about you. Sometimes you seem like yourself, but other times I hardly know you." Looking at me with those big brown eyes, wide with concern, he gave me a brotherly hug. "I'll be here when you're ready to talk."

On my eighteenth birthday, Mom and Dad took me to dinner at Sky City, a swanky restaurant in Seattle perched on top of the Space Needle. Kurt had a date so he couldn't come. The three of us sat up in the clouds, revolving ever so slowly.

Mom began talking about how the world just keeps turning and time marches on. She said that looking at Kurt and me reminded her of the song in *Fiddler on the Roof,* "Sunrise, Sunset." I was afraid she was going to start singing, *When did she get to be a beauty . . . when did he grow to be so tall . . . wasn't it yesterday that they were smaaall?*

• • • • •

Carly stopped to take a sip of Emma's chai tea. Then she looked at us, her eyes brimming with tears, and said, "I love my folks. They're a little corny, but they are decent, upstanding people and they love us kids wildly. I wanted them to be proud of me but feared the worst if they ever learned of my abortion. In fact, I didn't tell them for years. But on my eighteenth birthday, all I could think about was how lucky I was to be so loved." Carly wiped her eyes and blew her nose before continuing.

• • • • •

After stuffing ourselves on smoked salmon, we ordered coffee and watched the lights of Seattle shimmering off Puget Sound.

This is a nice way to celebrate my birthday, I thought. *There was a time not so long ago when I felt I had to be in the middle of my friends to have fun. Now I enjoy just being with my folks.*

"Better get going," Dad said. "Morning comes early."

"But, Dad," I objected. "It's only eight o'clock."

"I know, honey, but I promised Uncle Jim I'd go fishing with him in the morning and he's coming by to pick me up at four-thirty."

We found the car and were back in the neighborhood before 8:30. Mom was just finishing up the chorus of "Sunrise, Sunset" as we entered our street. The house was dark, but somewhere nearby, someone must have been having a party because there were cars everywhere.

As we opened the front door, you guessed it—a chorus of "Happy Birthday to You!" filled the living room. Kelly ran up and kissed me. Kurt and his girlfriend, Beth, gave me hugs and high fives. All my old girlfriends were there, including some who had seemed distant for a while. Many of Kurt's good-looking friends were there, too. Perhaps that explained why all the girls had shown up.

There was a new face there, a friend Kurt had met at Seattle Pacific University. His name was Joe and he had transferred from a Bible college in Tennessee. I decided that this was one boy I wanted to avoid even if he was a friend of Kurt's . . . and even if he was incredibly tall, dark, and handsome. I felt certain that kids from Bible college have extrasensory perception about evil. He'd somehow know about my abortion. What if he told Kurt? What if Kurt told Mom and Dad?

I found myself spending much of the evening just trying to stay out of his way.

A couple of days later Kurt asked me if I had met Joe at the party. When I told him I hadn't, Kurt asked what I thought of him.

"How can I think anything about him when I haven't even met him?"

"Well, did you at least see him? Did you think he was good looking?"

"I suppose so. If he's your friend, he'd have to be good-looking, because all of you guys are such studs!"

Kurt laughed. But then he added, "So, do you want to meet him?"

"No. Why?"

"Because he wants to meet you."

I'm thinking *Oh, great!* but said, "I'm not in the mood to meet anyone new these days. I'm just enjoying being with my old friends and my family. That's enough for me right now."

"You sure?" Kurt looked at me with something like confusion in his eyes.

"Yep, I'm sure." Much as I wanted to make my brother happy, I wasn't about to risk detection by this Bible thumper.

"Okay, but you're missing out on meeting a great guy."

"What is this?" I said, hands on hips. "Usually you're trying to keep your friends away from me."

"I know," Kurt said with a curious smile. "Funny, isn't it?"

"Well, anyway, I'm not interested."

"You're my kid sister. Whatever you say goes."

A week or so later, I was shopping in downtown Seattle when I ran into the Bible scholar from Tennessee. Joe recognized me first and came toward me with a grin and an outstretched hand.

"Hi, Birthday Girl. I'm Joe Collins, a friend of Kurt's. I didn't get a chance to meet you at your party. How about letting me buy you a belated birthday present, a cuppa joe?"

"How can I refuse?" I said. I couldn't think fast enough to come up with any plausible excuse. I did have time to notice the twinkle in his eyes.

"All right, then!" Joe smiled and nodded at a nearby coffee shop. "This one all right?"

"Sure, but I haven't got long. I need to be somewhere in twenty minutes." I lied. I don't lie ordinarily.

"Somewhere nearby?"

"About ten minutes from here." A lie compounded!

"Well, that gives us ten minutes to get acquainted. Guess we'd better talk fast." Joe laughed. "You want to sit inside or out here in the sun?"

"Inside," I said. "The exhaust fumes will spoil the coffee."

"Spoken like a true coffee lover," Joe said, holding open the door for me.

"What are you doing here in Seattle? Kurt told me you were from Tennessee."

"Yes. Tennessee is my home, but I'm just following orders from up above, and I'm certain that those orders include a stint in Seattle, Washington."

"Orders from up above?" Right then I made up my mind: I didn't like him. *Who's he trying to kid . . . like he gets his marching orders directly from God?* Those were my thoughts anyway. *And what's with his corny accent? God probably can't even understand him.*

"I'm just kidding you, Carly. You don't mind if I kid you, do you?" We ordered our drinks and sat down at a small bistro table. "Seriously though," he said, "I do try to listen to God and follow his instructions. And, from what Kurt has said, you and your family are also believers."

I drawled, "We ah believers indeed, Mistah Collins." Then taking a sip of my drink, I added, "And I do believe this cawffee is hawt!"

Instead of resenting my mockery, Joe laughed. "Now who's a jokester? You have a fine sense of humor, Carly."

It's strange. All my life I'd wanted to be clever. Kurt is funny. Mom and Dad are hilarious. But no one had ever thought me funny . . . till now.

Then I quickly reminded myself that there was nothing funny about my abortion and I had better be careful not to meet Joe's eyes. He'd certainly see right through me. After some chit-chat I excused myself to go to my so-called meeting, and that was all I heard from Joe for several months.

• • • • •

Later I learned from Kurt that Joe's dad had passed away. Joe had returned to Tennessee for the funeral and stayed to help his mom tie up some loose ends. By the time he returned to Seattle, I had already faced an important milestone in my life—the one-year anniversary of my abortion.

That was a difficult day for me, as it is for most post-abortive women. I kept thinking that if the baby had lived, she would now be about six months old. (I say "she" because I feel deep in my heart, the baby was a girl. I've given her the name "Grace" because I pray she'll have the grace to forgive me.)

I spent most of that sad day alone. Late morning I drove to Snohomish and poked through antique stores, picking up this or that treasure and then putting it down again. *What right do you have to buy treasures for yourself when you denied your little Grace the gift of life?*

Driving home, I heard a voice inside my head urging me to drive off the road or veer into an oncoming semi. *Why should you live when Grace is dead?* The voice became stronger and stronger with each passing mile. *Go faster! Drive off the bluff! You are a murderer and don't deserve to live!*

Through blinding tears, I tried to keep up with traffic, tried to stay on the road, tried to block the sneering voice from my thoughts. Sobs shook my body, and chills ran up and down my spine. *Yes, it's true. I don't deserve to live. I can end it all so easily. No one will know. It will seem like an accident.*

Just then I felt a force take the steering wheel and guide me off to the side of the road—to safety. No one can convince me it wasn't the hand of my Father God protecting me from harm. Despite my sin, he still loved me. That alone gave me reason to hope, reason to go on living. I banished all thought of suicide from my mind—shocked at how attractive that option had looked to me, a Christian.

Most anyone who's had an abortion knows that it's common for guilt to return with a vengeance on the anniversary of the abortion or on the baby's predicted birth date. Just getting through these landmark days can be a challenge. And usually, there's not a soul in the world who even knows what's troubling you.

But I made it through that first year and on into the next. I had even taken an apartment closer to my new job at Frederick & Nelson's department store. Mom and Dad weren't excited about my leaving the nest, but Kurt helped convince them. Since the apartment I'd chosen was only two blocks from his new place, he promised to keep an eye on me.

Working in the Junior Department at Frederick & Nelson's was a dream job. I loved their clothes and got an employee discount on anything I bought. My wardrobe never looked so good.

Each night I would come home to my new apartment, hang my lovely new clothes in the closet, slip something frozen into the microwave, pour myself a glass of something cold, eat, stretch out on the couch, and fall fast asleep for a couple of hours. Too much excitement, I guess.

One evening the doorbell rang just loud enough to wake me but not loud enough to *really* wake me, if you know what I mean. I stumbled to the door and opened it, without looking through the peephole.

Lucky for me, it was Kurt. He was with someone else, but I couldn't see who it was through the fog in my head.

"Who are you, and what do you want?" I murmured to the stranger.

"I'm Joe, Carly. Joe Collins? Cuppa Joe? Friend of Kurt's."

"Any friend of Kurt's is a cuppa joe," I murmured.

"Carly, have you been drinking?" Kurt asked, taking me by the shoulders.

"No way, man! She was telling a joke. That's a good one, Carly; you're so funny."

Kurt and I stared at Joe. But, deep inside, I liked it that at least someone in the world thought I was funny, even though I hadn't meant to be.

Giving me a sidelong glance, Kurt said, "Carly, get yourself together and come with us to Pike's Market. Can you believe Joe's never been there?"

"What's so big about going to a fish market?" Joe said, adding, "but I'd sure like to have you join us, Carly."

And so I shook the fog from my head, put on one of my new outfits, and went with my brother and his friend to the Pike Place Public Market.

In the car, Joe told us about his trip to Tennessee, his father's funeral, his mother's business affairs, and his decision to return to Seattle. "I like to finish what I start," Joe said, "and I have some unfinished business here in Seattle."

"Like finishing school?" I asked.

"That and a couple of other things."

"What courses are you taking, Joe?" I asked, though I was really wondering what other unfinished business he had in Seattle.

"I'm studying theology, want to be a pastor one day. What do you think of ol' Cuppa Joe being a pastor?"

"You don't look like a pastor," I said, fumbling for words. Now I was really worried. A pastor would never understand my abortion, not in a million years! I'd better keep my head down and my guard up.

"Here we are," Kurt proclaimed. "Thank God for a parking space!"

I was thanking God, too. Now we could talk about something else.

Since Joe hadn't been to Pike's Market before, Kurt and I decided to have a little fun at his expense. As we strolled down the Main Arcade, gawking at the vast variety of foods and wares, we heard some shouting. Kurt winked at me, and we ducked just as a salmon flew past us. Unprepared, Joe nearly got smacked in the face as the fish monger threw a second salmon across the aisle to his buddy.

In his Southern accent, Joe bellowed, "Glory be! Fish ah jumping and the cotton is high."

We laughed till our sides ached. Just thinking about it makes me laugh today! Joe was a good sport, lots of fun, and it did seem to me that he was even more handsome than when I first saw him at my party nearly two years before. But there was that troublesome part about his becoming a pastor.

When Kurt and Joe took me home, we made plans for the three of us to spend the day together at the park on Saturday, throwing Frisbees and just hanging out. I remember thinking how nice it was of Kurt to include me in the fun.

Kurt asked Beth at the last minute, so we became a foursome. It wasn't like a date, just a bunch of friends spending time together. At the end of the day, Joe walked me to the door while Kurt and Beth discussed the relative merits of Frisbees and hula hoops.

As I dug in my purse for the house key, Joe asked if I'd like to go sailing with him the following Saturday.

"Well . . . sounds like fun, Joe, but I . . . uh, I . . . I think I have something planned for next Saturday. Yes, I do."

Joe looked discouraged but was apparently not going to be put off so easily. "Can you cancel it?"

"And why would I do that?"

"Because I'd really like to spend the day with you, get to know you better . . . and I'd like you to get to know me better, too, so that . . ."

"So that what?"

"Well, you know, so that we could see if there is any chemistry, any future, for us." Joe looked at his feet, then back up into my face. He was smiling.

"Oh, Joe. I don't think so," I said, looking away.

"Well, why not?"

"I don't know you well enough to tell you why not." I remember thinking *what is it about "no" you don't understand?*

"Is it something about me?" Joe looked into my eyes. "You won't hurt my feelings. Maybe it's something I can change." He was so sweet and humble. I could see why Kurt liked him.

"Oh, no, Joe. It's nothing like that."

"Well then, what?"

Will he never let up? I thought. "It's nothing. It's . . . nothing." Fumbling in vain for a reason that would satisfy Joe, I finally gave in. "Yes, yes, I'll go sailing with you on Saturday."

"Well, good! That's good. I'll pick you up at 9:30 A.M., sharp. OK?"

"Yes. Okay. I'll be ready." *What am I getting myself into?*

With that, Joe touched me lightly on the cheek and bounded down the stairs to Kurt and Beth.

My week at Frederick & Nelson's dragged, not so much because I was anxious to see Joe but because I was curious about him. I liked him, and I felt safe with him. But he could never like someone who'd done what I had done. And even if he could forgive me, he was going to be a pastor.

Like the Sword of Damocles, the guilt was always there, hanging over my head. I had done a terrible thing, no question about it, and I could never undo what I had done. But what about this guilt? How would I get rid of it? Would my soul be in torment all my life? *Well, and why not? You took the life of your baby.*

There it was again. I'd been a fool to agree to see Joe. I had no right to think of having fun, no right at all. Maybe I should call him in the morning and cancel.

But I didn't cancel. Joe was at my doorstep at 9:30 A.M., sharp, and I was ready.

"I wasn't sure what to wear. Do I look okay?"

Joe gave me the once over. "You look great, Carly. Better than great. You're beautiful." Then, as if embarrassed, he changed the subject. "Have you ever been sailing before?"

"No. This is a first."

"Then I'm going to make it a priority to guarantee you have a good time. There's nothing like sailing for getting the heart rate up. It's a thrill a minute." Joe smiled, took my sweater from me, and placed it on my shoulders. "Let's go!"

"The weather's perfect for sailing," he said, as we approached the Port of Everett. "There's a sailing club here, lots of beautiful sailboats. But I'm just a renter, a weekend boater with grand ambitions to one day be a sailboat captain."

"I thought you wanted to be a pastor."

"Yes, a fisher of men." Then with a sly grin, he added, "Doesn't that suggest I'm going to need a boat?"

"Whatever you say, Cuppa Joe, or should I call you Cuppa Sloop?"

Joe laughed as if I had just cracked the joke of the century. "Cuppa Sloop! That's another good one, Carly." Shaking his head with delight, Joe grinned.

As we approached the sailing club, my heart leaped. Dozens of beautiful vessels bobbed side by side, just waiting for someone to take them out. Off in the distance, dotted here and there, were spectacular boats with sails unfurled, skimming the deep blue waters of Puget Sound.

Joe made arrangements and we went down to the dock to board our sailboat. It was a nice one—as far as I could tell. Joe seemed to know exactly what he was doing, so I found a seat and began putting on sunscreen. Sunlight sparkled on the rippling wake left by other small boats coming and going to the dock.

"Okay, Carly. We're off. Why don't you just sit right over here so you won't get hit by the boom."

We didn't talk much. Joe did what he needed to do to get us away from shore and out onto the Sound. Then the wind caught the sail and we were on our way. It was glorious—the breezes, the salt sea air, the gulls. I heard laughter and realized it was me, giggling without reservation at the sheer delight of sailing with the wind.

A time or two the sails slackened and Joe came back to sit with me. "You having a good time?"

"The best! I had no idea how much fun sailing was!" I licked the salt from my lips while brushing hair back from my eyes. And then I was all questions. How long had he been sailing? Where did he learn? Are there schools to teach such things or did a friend teach him? Can anybody rent a sailboat or is there some kind of certification, like a driver's license, that you have to present?

"Slow down . . . slow down. I'll answer all those questions once you come up for air." Grabbing my hand, he put a finger to my lips.

"I guess I've been sailing five or six years." He'd gone to a sailing school in Nashville on J. Percy Priest Lake where they offer classroom and on-the-water training. He'd taken basic training and loved it so much that he kept going through advanced levels of seamanship and boat handling. "Ended up getting my ASA certification. So now I can rent a sailboat wherever I go."

"Wow!" I exclaimed. "Well, anytime you're looking for someone to take with you, count me in. This is the most . . ." And before I could say another word, the wind picked up and Joe was up and away to tend the sails.

I was going to say, "This is the most exciting thing I've ever done." Was it? Was it more exciting than sitting behind Eric on the motorcycle, my mind exploring different possibilities, most of which were not wise or good or acceptable?

When I went out with Eric, the excitement was tinged with lustful thoughts and sensual desires. It never felt right and it never felt good. Boating with Joe, on the other hand, was good, clean, exciting fun. He treated me with respect and dignity. I could tell he liked me but he didn't try anything. He was a gentleman. *He is way too good for me. I don't deserve anyone like Joe.*

As we docked the boat and signed her back in, Joe said, "How about some lunch?"

"Sure, Joe, I'll bet you're hungry. What you were doing looked like a lot of hard work."

"Sailing has made me the muscle-bound chap that I am," Joe laughed. I had to admit he was buff.

We drove to Ivar's on Pier 54 and ordered fish and chips along with clam chowder. After dinner, we sat and enjoyed watching the boats glide past, some destined for romantic islands and beyond . . . to Victoria, B.C.

"Have you been to the San Juans?" I asked.

"Yes," Joe said, running his finger around his water glass, making tracks in the evaporation. "A friend and I took our bikes on the ferry and island-hopped. It was a beautiful way to see this remarkable piece of God's country."

"Our family has done that, too. I loved it."

"What else do you love, Carly?"

I sensed the conversation taking a turn but refused to get serious. "I love butterflies," I said, fluttering my eyelids, "the white ones that skim the lavender in Mom's herb garden. I love my family, my friends . . . love to write, poems mostly . . . love soccer, and now I love sailing!"

Joe continued to probe. "What are your goals? Future plans?"

"Seriously?" I laughed, hoping to keep the conversation and our friendship superficial.

"Seriously."

I twisted my napkin, buying some time. "I haven't thought too much about goals. I know I don't want to stay at Frederick & Nelson's forever, though I do love working there. I like helping people. And future plans?" I shrugged. "It's hard to have future plans when you haven't really nailed down any goals."

"Good answers." He nodded, then cleared his throat and looked steadily at me. "How do you feel about marriage and children? Do you see babies in your future?"

"Oh . . . babies." I tried to think fast. *Don't look at Joe. Mustn't let him see my eyes, windows to the soul. He mustn't know about the baby.* "Um, well, let me think. Um, yes, babies are . . . ."

And then suddenly a wave of panic, hysteria—something—flooded over me. Breaking out in a sweat I tried to excuse myself, but words wouldn't come. Joe looked at me quizzically as I rushed past him to the ladies' room, found a chair, sat down, counted to ten, stuffed my sweater over my mouth to muffle my groans, and wept like I'd never wept before.

One woman asked if she could help. Another asked if I needed anything or anyone. To both, I shook my head. *Nothing, and no one can help. My past has caught up to my present and is overtaking my future. There will be no babies, no happiness for me. I have killed my future; I will never outrun my past.*

Apparently, one of the women told the hostess about me and next thing I knew she was in the powder room trying to comfort me. She asked if I was alone or with someone.

That brought me back to reality—fast! *Joe. I'd left Joe out there. He must be wondering if I ran out on him. He must think I'm nuts. Wash your face. Do something about those puffy eyes.*

I described Joe to the hostess and asked her to tell him to meet me at the car in a few minutes. Quickly, I splashed cold water on my eyes, washed my face, and left for the parking lot. Joe was waiting beside the car.

"Carly, are you all right? What happened?"

"Joe, can we just not talk about it?" I took his hand and tried to look at him. "I want to thank you for a wonderful day, but I'd like to go home now."

"But, Carly. I must have said something. I have to know what it was so I won't upset you again. Next time I'll be more careful."

I looked him squarely in the face. "Joe, there won't be a next time. You are terrific. Any girl would be lucky to have you for a friend, but—not me. You are not for me. And I am definitely not for you."

Joe took me by the shoulders, looked deep into my eyes, and pleaded, "What is it?"

Wait a minute, I thought. *He's looking into my eyes, into my soul, and he can't see my guilt. Maybe we could build a relationship after all. He wouldn't ever have to know.*

As soon as I thought it, I knew it was wrong. Joe was too decent, too honest for me to deceive. But I wasn't sure about telling him the truth. I was so confused, my thoughts raced. *Once he knows the truth he won't want me anymore. But, of course, I don't deserve him anyway. If I tell him, at least he'll understand why we can't be together. He'll know that he hasn't done anything wrong, that I'm the one with the problem. Poor sweet Joe . . . .*

Again Joe asked, "What is it, Carly?"

I took his hand and led him to a secluded bench on the waterfront. Not daring to look at him, I told Joe the whole sorry story with my eyes fixed on the gravel path. As I finished, I expected to hear footsteps walking away from me; but, instead, Joe took me in his arms and held me close.

Quietly he spoke. "I am so sorry that happened, Carly, so very sorry. I promise I will do my best to protect you, if you'll let me. I won't let anything bad happen to you again."

I started to cry. Who was this man—that he should love me? He knew what I had done to Grace, but he promised to protect me. Me! We cried together and those tears sealed a bond between us that has kept us to this day.

• • • • •

Emma shrieked. "Carly, you got the perfect man!"

Carly smiled. "Joe would be the first one to say he isn't perfect. Like everyone, he has his flaws . . . but what I love about him is his sincerity, his kindness. He's still that way to me and to our daughters."

"When you told him your story that day, did you tell him all about Eric?" Mariah asked. Then she lowered her eyes, as if embarrassed to have asked such a personal question.

"Only part of it, and we agreed that was in the past. We haven't discussed Eric since."

"Did you get engaged right away?" Emma's eyes were wide as silver dollars.

"We were married within six months," Carly answered. "I got pregnant on our honeymoon."

"Do you mind my asking something personal, Carly? It's something I've often wondered about," Emma asked.

"Go for it. I'll answer if I can."

"Did getting pregnant with a baby you wanted cause you to relive your abortion and all that led up to it?"

Annie gave Emma a disapproving look.

Emma lowered her eyes. "I'm sorry, Carly. I knew I shouldn't have asked that. It was too personal, probably too painful."

"No, that's okay, really. I get asked that question almost every time I tell my story. And the answer is yes, quite frankly, carrying a wanted baby did bring back sad memories. But those painful memories led me to the healing I needed to outdistance my past."

"Tell us about that, Carly," Annie said.

• • • • •

Well, when I suspected I was pregnant, I visited our local pregnancy center for a free pregnancy test. With Joe still in school, money was tight. Anyway, as part of the intake procedure, the counselor asked if I'd had any previous pregnancies, and, if so, what was the outcome? When I told her I had aborted my first child, she asked how I felt about that.

I told her I wasn't doing well at all, that I needed help. That's when she told me about the H.E.A.R.T. groups using material from the book *Forgiven and Set Free,* by Linda Cochrane.

Anyway, working through these issues with others who had gone through them put things into perspective. I learned to accept God's forgiveness and to forgive myself. That's why I'm such a firm believer in these groups and why I began facilitating them years ago.

Watching you release your balloons today took me back eight years to the day I released my balloon for Grace, my firstborn. I believe she has forgiven me for not wanting her. I want her so much now. I know I will see her again—in heaven.

Sometimes it helps me to visit the Memorial for the Unborn in Newberg where I placed a plaque in memory of Grace. I like to go there by myself, sit on the bench, and talk to God about her. I ask him to hold her for me and to tell her how much I love her.

I know that you're all still hurting, especially you, Emma, because your grief is fresh. But I do want to assure you that God loves you and he will help you through the rest of your days. You've joined the ranks of those who have been forgiven and set free. I love you and am glad to call you my friends.

"We love you too, Carly," shouted a chorus of voices.

"Let's take a break," Emma said. "The bathroom is down the hall."

• • • • •

After our break Annie said, "I'm terribly sorry, but I'm going to need to leave. I forgot I have an appointment in the morning and I need my beauty sleep more than ever now I've passed fifty."

"Tell me about it," I said, laughing. "I wonder if we shouldn't all call it a day. It's late, and people have to work in the morning." I paused. "You know, just because our support group is formally coming to a close doesn't mean we can't meet—as friends. Why don't we continue to meet at my coffee shop on Wednesday nights? Business is usually slow on Wednesday nights anyway . . . I don't mind closing up early—not for something as good as our times together."

"So then we could continue to tell the long versions of our stories next Wednesday night," Carly said.

"And continue as long as it takes," I added.

"Sounds good!" said Annie. "I don't want to miss anything."

I didn't want to miss anything either. Going home that night, I found Bill asleep in his recliner, remote in hand. *Darling Bill, the television news must have put you to sleep. You should have been with me. Carly's story would have kept you wide awake. I'll have to find a way for you to get to know these friends of mine.*

• • • • •

In the morning, I opened the coffee shop and hit the ground running—customers dashing in out of the rain for a java jolt and a muffin to start their day. By mid morning, it was just me, my thoughts, and a floor that badly needed mopping. While I mopped, I thought about Carly.

Throughout the week, Carly's story continued to dominate my thoughts. I admired the way she was able to move on with her life. It seemed she truly had forgiven herself. *That's the hard part—forgiving yourself. But Carly has it all together, if she's being real with us.*

When I came to faith and asked God's forgiveness all those years ago, I truly believe he forgave me. And I was glad for it! But I can't seem to forgive myself. After all this time, I still hear inner voices of condemnation. "What kind of a mother would abandon her child in his hour of need?" How those voices scald my heart!

• • • • •

"Hey, wake up, Dreamer. Maybe you need a shot of your own caffeine." It was Emma.

"Hi, Sweetie. I didn't hear you come in. You want the usual?"

"Yup, with skim milk, please. I've been waiting for this all day."

"Double caramel?"

"Of course. That's why the skim milk," she winked. "Wasn't Carly's story amazing? I haven't been able to think of anything else. I wonder whatever happened to Eric. I hope Carly can find out. You know we're supposed to help her."

"I felt so sorry for him . . . for both of them really. I mean I can see how a young girl with a complex could fall for someone who is a little edgy, a little dangerous."

"Just think, Liz. She might have married Eric out of sympathy or desperation. Where would she be today?"

"I'm sure women have done that, and lived miserably ever after. It was wise of Carly to realize that it was lust, not love, at least on her part. And who knows if Eric even knew the meaning of love, poor fellow, growing up in the home that he did."

"That mother of his! What a great example she was!" Emma grimaced.

I'd been thinking about Eric's mother. True, she was screwed up. Yet, she'd been dealt a blow by her husband—leaving her to raise three boys all alone. It's difficult to judge someone when you haven't walked in her shoes. So I simply responded, "It was a mess, and Eric got caught in the middle of it."

"Joe was his polar opposite. What a neat guy, about as close to perfect as possible. And he really fell for Carly. I wish someone nice like that, and cute, would fall for me." Emma put her hands together, prayer fashion.

"Oh, Emma, I'm sure you've had lots of cute boys after you."

"But who wants a boy, Liz? I want a man, someone cute who is also mature, wise—and rich—to fall head over heels for me, the way Joe did for Carly. Someone who will take me in his arms and tell me that he is sorry for every bad thing that has ever happened to me and will promise to protect me forever."

"That sounds wonderful, all right."

"What about you, Liz? You're married."

"Yes. I've been married over thirty-five years—to the same man."

Emma's eyes widened, her head rolling down and forward. "Thirty-five years! Was he like Joe? Did he treat you like a queen? Was he everything you ever dreamed of and that's why you fell in love?" Emma was like a little girl hammering questions at her mother.

"You know, it's hard to remember that far back. Let's put it this way. Bill is *now* almost everything I ever dreamed of. It took awhile for both of us to grow up and get to this point."

"It wasn't perfect, yet you stuck it out for thirty-five years?"

"Of course, Emma. Why should that seem strange? That's what marriage vows are all about . . . till death do us part. And the good news, at least for Bill and me, is that every year seems better than the year before. I adore my husband, but it hasn't always been that way. I'm just glad we didn't throw in the towel those times when we were really tempted to give up."

Emma looked amazed. I don't wonder. Her generation has grown up with divorce being commonplace. Fidelity and longevity seem to be rare in marriages today.

"I've been waiting for Mr. Perfect to come along. All my friends are, too—we're in no hurry. But the longer I look for Mr. Perfect, the more I wonder if he's out there at all. And what if I find him only to discover he thinks he's too good for me?"

"Then he wouldn't be perfect, Emma. He'd be proud. Anyway, nobody's perfect."

Emma looked at me with those big brown eyes of hers. How could you not love Emma? She is so totally . . . Emma.

"Deep down, I know that. I just don't want to saddle myself with the wrong person. Is that selfish, Liz?"

"Not at all. It's one of the most important decisions you'll ever make. Naturally, you want to choose well. I think you'll know when Mr. Right comes along. You'll love him in spite of the fact he's not Mr. Perfect."

"In the meantime, I've got a great job and lots of good friends," Emma sighed.

"Sounds like a happy life to me."

Emma's face grew serious. "Most of the time. But I'm so glad for this H.E.A.R.T. group. It's helping me work through my guilty feelings about the abortion."

"That's the point, isn't it? Guilt is no friend to anybody—always hanging around and making us miserable."

"Has H.E.A.R.T. helped you with your guilt, Liz? What about your little boy? How old would he be now?"

Before I could answer, a young couple walked in and sauntered dreamily, hand-in-hand, up to the counter. Emma caught my eye with a raised eyebrow and slipped out the door singing, *"Someday, my prince will come."*

By closing time, I was exhausted and had a splitting headache. All afternoon Emma's question ran through my mind. "Has H.E.A.R.T. helped you with your guilt, Liz?"

Frankly, no! I'd hoped it would, but I had doubts from the very beginning that anything could take away my guilt after all these years. Jeremy would be thirty years old now. For thirty years I've lived with guilt instead of with my son. Hardly a fair exchange! But what right does an unfit mother have to expect fairness?

Bill gets mad at me when I talk about being an unfit mother. He says if I'm an unfit mother, then that makes him an unfit father, and he doesn't think that's true. He says we made our choice based on the information we had at the time. But the information was wrong, all wrong, and we should have known that. We should have gotten a second opinion! The fact that we didn't plagues me to this day.

Bill points to our two daughters as evidence of what a good mother I am. He says I was a model parent to those girls and points out all sorts of reasons why this is so. I say "Phooey, if I was such a good mother, why does Joy hardly speak to me?" He can't answer that. So, much as I'd like to believe him, I still see myself as unfit. An unfit mother.

Maybe I'll tell the long version of my story next Wednesday. Get it over with. See if Carly can come up with some magic potion to change the way I feel. I hope she can.

CHAPTER FOUR

ANNIE'S TRIP TO HAIGHT-ASHBURY

By the time we met on Wednesday, I had braced myself. This was the night. I would tell all. Perhaps I'd begin to feel—what is it that Carly says?—*"forgiven and set free."* Free from the label engraved on my heart . . . unfit mother.

We started late as it took some time to usher my lingering customers out the door, put on fresh coffee for the group, and get everyone settled. Then there was an unexpected phone call, and by the time I got back to the group, Annie had taken the floor.

Disappointed, I sat down and listened to Annie tell her story.

• • • • •

You all know that I had an abortion way back when. You may not know that I am fifty-five years old (because I look so young!) and getting a few gray hairs (because I touch them up!) Now that you know all of this, you may be wondering what an old broad like me could possibly have to share with anyone, especially young women at a pregnancy center. Well, I'm going to tell you.

I love the girls who come into the center. Many of them remind me of my own troubled youth. I'd have given anything to have had a pregnancy center to come to when I was wrestling with my own decision. So I work there, figuring I'm doing what I can to keep the doors open for today's young women.

As for my personal story, I grew up in the 1960s, a flower child. Oh, and so cute I was! My friends and I wore the wildest outfits, ranging from granny dresses—braless, of course—to men's overalls to go-go-dresses with go-go boots. We found most of our clothing at second-hand thrift stores or army surplus stores. The guys wore bell bottom jeans and tie-dyed shirts.

The clothes we wore shocked our parents who had lived through the Depression and were determined that their families would never wear tattered clothing again.

Most of us wore our hair long, either hanging down straight or in the wildest afros. Me? I could do both. I'd straighten it for the long gaunt look, then step outside into the morning fog and it would go all curly on me. I could be Cher one minute and Little Orphan Annie the next. Oh, but it didn't matter: long hair, wild hair—they were both "in."

We were in rebellion—against our parents, authority figures, and the Vietnam War. Since the U.S. Army required our guys to wear crew cuts, we figured long, unruly hair was the appropriate response for us to have. We also favored bright colors in contrast to the drab olive green uniforms that soldiers wore.

Our symbol was a peace sign, or a dove. Our sayings were, "Groovy!" "Can you dig it?" "Right on!" and "If it feels good, do it!" Our slogan was, "Make love, not war." And we did. Make love, I mean. I learned this up close and personal when I left home at the age of eighteen.

My family lived outside of San Francisco, and on one of our trips to town, I asked if we could drive by the Haight-Ashbury District. Even my Dad was curious about the doings around San Francisco State College so he agreed. Holey, moley, I couldn't believe my eyes. It was bizarre. Beyond bizarre. But this eighteen-year-old wanted to see it up closer.

The following weekend my friend Rachel and I returned, parked her VW Beetle and didn't go back home for nearly a year.

Within the first half hour of our arrival, we were "picked up" by a group of flower children carrying signs that read, "Free love and equality for all." The girls and guys wore peace signs around their necks and rainbow tattoos on their shoulders. Some wore flowers in their hair.

"Come. Join us in our quest for peace."

"Sounds like fun," Rachel said. I agreed, so we joined the quest.

We walked all over The Haight, talking to tourists and recruiting other young people until nightfall. As Rachel and I prepared to return to the car, one of the group "leaders" named Jimi—after his idol Jimi Hendrix—said, "Hey, why don't you stay with us?"

"Yes. Stay with us," a chorus of voices added.

"I guess we could stay the night," I said. "Let me call my folks." You should have seen the looks I got, like I had just arrived from Mars. "Just to let them know I won't be home tonight. So they won't worry." More looks.

Then Jimi spoke up, "Groovy!"

"Yeah, groovy!" the chorus chimed in.

As it turned out, Rachel and I spent that night, and the next. At the end of the week we decided to make our home right there in The Haight with our new friends in their "cash pad" (That's what they called their place, I don't know why. It was a dilapidated old house that had been vacant for, probably, twenty years).

With no rent to pay, we could make ends meet by panhandling and bartering for what we needed. Rachel and I quickly learned that since our hippy friends had a liberal viewpoint when it came to sex, lovemaking was just another commodity to trade for food and necessities. Much as Rachel and I initially felt like prostitutes, we soon accepted even this as part of the lifestyle we'd chosen and chanted heartily along with the crowd, "Make love, not war!"

One day I met a guy on the corner of Haight and Stanyan who invited me to his apartment. He was older, looked like a professor with long graying hair—but he wore ratty jeans along with a black T-shirt and tweed sport coat. He said he wanted to barter for sex. I said okay and followed him to his place near San Francisco State.

He asked me if I did drugs. I said no, drugs did not appeal to me.

"Far out," was all he said. After we had sex, he proceeded to lecture me on the fine art of bartering. Always agree in advance what the trade will be. He had no money—nor any food to trade—only drugs. Take it or leave it. Then his face softened.

"Look, I like you. I'd like to meet you again, soon and often. What's your problem with drugs?"

"I don't like the way my friends act when they're smoking pot."

"Well, of course, you're talking pot. What I'm talking about is something altogether different. This is a mind-expanding drug, psychedelic. You'll see the world with a whole new set of eyes. Everything is beautiful, exciting, bigger than life."

"I don't think so." I shook my head. "I don't know what you're talking about."

"You've never heard of LSD?" he said in a mocking tone.

"Well, maybe once or twice," I said, embarrassed to look ridiculous in this man's eyes—this man who owed me money! "Anyway, you owe me cash, not some crazy drug."

"No money. LSD yes, money no." I left without cash and with diminishing self-respect.

When I got back to the house, I told Jimi and Rachel what happened.

Jimi looked at me in amazement. "You had a chance to get some LSD and you turned it down?"

"I didn't want LSD. I wanted money. We need groceries."

"*You* want groceries! The rest of us would have been glad to get the LSD. But you ended up with nothing. Maybe that's all you're worth."

I left the room in tears. *How dare he speak to me that way?* Rachel came in and put her arms around me. "He didn't mean it, Annie. He's just upset. Come on. Let's get ready to go."

"Go where? I thought we got to stay home tonight."

"We're going to a party. It'll be fun. Jimi says there will be some far-out happenings, new people."

"Jimi says—with you lately, it's always Jimi this, Jimi that."

"Don't be that way, Annie. It'll be fun. You'll see."

And so we went to yet another party. Far-out happenings? I'll say. Someone brought LSD, and soon everyone except me was "dropping acid and getting stoned." Looking around, I saw expressions of ecstasy on many faces—and horror on others. Curious, I wanted to try it; yet something held me back. Then, I did what Dad always told me to do if I got into a tight spot. I called a cab and went home . . . well, not home, really. I went to the cash pad.

In the morning Rachel kept talking about the "trip" she had been on. She called me stupid for not having tried it. She said I should either become one spirit with her and the others or hit the highway. *What happened to make love, not war? What about free love? It seemed to me that free love meant giving my body away freely so Jimi and the rest could smoke pot and drop acid.*

I decided to call Dad and ask him to come and pick me up, take me home. Though I hadn't contacted the family for several months, Dad asked no questions. He simply said, "I'm on my way. Stay put till I get there."

• • • • •

Two weeks after our tearful family reunion, I realized I had skipped my period. I didn't know what to do and even thought that if I concentrated real hard, I could will the problem away. No good. I skipped another period.

What could I do? Where could I go? Who would I tell? If I told my parents, they'd probably closet me away for nine months, or send me to a maternity home in another state. I couldn't claim I was raped; yet I also couldn't tell who the father was. There was simply no way of knowing since, sadly, there had been so many men.

Much as I hated myself for doing it, I fled back to San Francisco. If anyone would know what to do, Jimi would. He would know someone. He could tell me where to get this problem solved.

I must have been insane to trust Jimi, knowing him as I did. I won't go into the gruesome details, but Jimi did indeed know someone, someone who scraped out my insides so indelicately that I would never be able to have children.

• • • • •

Emma was the first to react. "No! No!" she cried, running to throw her arms around Annie. We all dissolved in tears, mixed with anger, that our friend—charming, funny, and full of life—had been deceived and damaged by those who claimed to have cornered the market on love.

My mind was churning. *This explains why she doesn't have any children. And why she never told me about her abortion. It would be way too painful.*

I shook my head, remembering the sixties. So much violence! So much hatred! In large sections of the population, themes of honor and respect for authority flew out the window along with morality and temperance. All in the name of love!

Annie looked at us one by one and continued.

• • • • •

All these years I've agonized over the lifestyle I lived in San Francisco, the baby I aborted as well as the other babies I was unable to have. Like Carly, I suffered from post-abortion stress, anger, and depression. I've always had a difficult time relating to men, even nice men. I've tended to see myself as a commodity to be bartered, rather than a person of value.

I've also had a hard time relating to children because whenever I see them, I remember what I did to my own child. Each and every time my sister Jill Marie would ask me to babysit her kids, I'd try any excuse I could think of to avoid it.

One day, Jill Marie called my bluff. "Annie, why do you avoid being around my children? Don't deny it now. It's true. You and I both know it."

I didn't know what to say. My precious sister was calling me out, calling me to confess. I tried saying I just felt uncomfortable around children, not having any of my own.

"I don't buy that, Annie. There's more to it, isn't there? I know you too well. I'm your sister; we know everything about each other—except this. I love you and want to know what's troubling you."

"I don't think I can tell you."

"Why not?"

"I don't think I'm ready to tell you."

"When will you be ready?"

"I don't know, possibly never." I hung my head, not wanting to meet her eyes.

"What?" she cried. "How can you say that to me? We're family. You're my big sister. I've never withheld anything from you. You are my confidante; you've helped me through every one of my tough times. Now you won't let me help you back?"

"Jill Marie . . . ." I reached out to her but she turned away.

"No! As much as I love you, I love my children. I want them to have a relationship with you . . . want them to know you. But they can't, because you won't let them. That's not fair, Annie, not fair to them or to me . . . or to you."

Jill Marie looked at me for the longest time, not saying a word, and then broke into tears, sobs racking her body. I'd never realized how much I meant to her, how much she cared about her kids spending time with me. Would I ever be able to meet her expectations? Could I learn to be around her children without remembering my own loss? *You'll have to learn,* I thought. *You'll have to do whatever you can to find some healing so you can go on with your life.*

I ended up telling Jill Marie that she was right, that I did indeed have a problem. I told her I absolutely loved her, as well as her children, and that I would do all I could to get well. I promised her I'd get professional help, and that I'd talk with her about it as soon as I could do so without falling apart.

"Oh, Annie, I just wish I could make you well, now . . . . I wish I could make things better for you."

"I do too, dearest, but this is a problem that cut me so deeply it won't stop bleeding without something strong."

• • • • •

Do you think I could find any professional counselor who would believe that an abortion could put me in such a state? Certainly not women counselors! I spoke to three of them over the years and they all felt that abortion was a "right" we should protect, that it leveled the playing field for women, and that any negative talk about its effects on women should be squelched. They always looked elsewhere for the source of my "psychosis."

The men counselors I talked with weren't any better. There hadn't been any long-term studies on the aftereffects of abortion, and they felt sure that the real answer lay deeply imbedded in other experiences, like possibly being molested as a child by my father. I wanted to puke. "If you only knew my father," I exploded to one of them, "you'd see how ridiculous, how shameful it is even to suggest that. I could throttle you for saying such a thing. You haven't heard a word I've said. Oh, what's the use?"

Anyway, Jill Marie's children grew up, and I never was able to reach out to them—such a pity, for all of us, but especially for me. I lost out on the chance to know those great kids, and I let my loving little sister down.

I did marry. George. He was a good man. Though I never told him about the abortion, he understood from the start that I was unable to have children, and he was willing to leave it at that. He was a good uncle to Jill Marie's children, filling in for me frequently when I just couldn't "rise to the occasion." I always regretted that I wasn't ever good in bed for George. He died ten years ago of a massive coronary.

• • • • •

Annie stopped and looked at us. We were crying. Her concern, as always, was for us—not for herself—never for herself. "Oh, I didn't mean to make you cry. I'm so sorry."

We encouraged her to continue . . . and she did.

• • • • •

Actually that's when my own healing began. I was seeking counseling because of George's sudden death and was referred to Dr. Roberts, an enlightened psychologist. She had read many articles published by The Elliot Institute, a group that studies the aftereffects of abortion on women. Dr. Roberts believed there could well be a connection between my abortion and the way I've felt ever since then. She walked me through the steps we have been studying in H.E.A.R.T. and I found partial healing and forgiveness. That was nine years ago.

Although I still find it difficult to relate to children, slowly my uneasiness around men began to dissipate. I also noticed that a load of guilt was lifted off my shoulders. I could breathe again, and the feelings of suffocation were gone. I was no longer bitter toward Rachel and Jimi and that entire period of my life. I was, as we say in H.E.A.R.T., forgiven and set free.

That's when I knew I had to share these truths with others. I learned about the pregnancy center movement and discovered there was a center not too far away in Santa Rosa where I could volunteer. I loved the work so much that as soon as a staff opening came up, I applied. After five years learning the ropes, I saw in a national pregnancy center magazine that there was an opening up here in the Portland area.

I was ready for a change and took the position of center director here in Portland. That's how I happen to know Liz. Her coffee shop became one of my favorite haunts on lunch breaks, a place to get a "jolt" so I could go back and face my world of suffering young women.

There couldn't be more meaningful work to do, for me anyway, than helping these young women who are undecided regarding their pregnancies. I know the feeling of facing an unexpected and unwanted pregnancy. However, I also know the devastation that abortion caused in my life and I want to help steer them away from the same dead end. That's my calling, I believe.

It's also my calling to help women who have been wounded through abortion by promoting H.E.A.R.T. groups. So when Liz asked me about post-abortion stress, I felt God had opened a door—the door of her coffee shop—to start a group right here in this neighborhood, to help bring healing to others who are post-abortive.

In the process, I've had the good fortune to meet all of you, to make new friends, friends I love.

That's my story . . . and I'm sticking to it.

• • • • •

"Wow, Annie, unbelievable!" Mariah was first to speak. "I hadn't heard what life was like for young people in the sixties."

Annie twinkled, "Bet you thought old gals like me never had a life."

"No," Mariah answered, fiddling with her glasses. "It's not that. I guess I've been so tuned in to my own hard times that I never thought about someone like you, someone so nice, having had to deal with mean people."

"Mean people are everywhere, Sweetie. You just can't let them rob you of the joy of living. Life is too short for that."

"You're a *groovy* chick, Annie," Emma winked.

"Far out," Annie responded, making the peace sign to Emma.

• • • • •

After everyone left that evening, I sat down at the counter with the rest of the biscotti and pondered something that Annie had said, "I also noticed that a load of guilt had been lifted off my shoulders . . . I had been forgiven and set free."

How, Annie, how? Why you and not me? Why can't I experience forgiveness no matter how desperately I try?

What is it about forgiveness? Why is it so elusive? The first time I heard about God's forgiveness—that he would forgive my sins if I simply believed on his Son Jesus—I shook my head. *It can't be that easy,* I thought. *What do I have to do? There's got to be some bloodletting.* And, of course, there was . . . but it was Christ's blood, not mine. I had to learn to apply God's forgiveness to my own situations. With God's help, I was able to do that. But how do I forgive myself?

All day Thursday, I pondered these things as, between customers, I deep-cleaned the shop . . . scrubbing behind canisters, polishing chrome fixtures, wiping down the walls, sterilizing stainless steel coffee measuring spoons. The place fairly shone!

On Friday, Carly surprised me with a visit.

"Hey, I'm going to make a regular customer out of you yet," I said. "What can I get for you?"

She laughed, her eyes sparkling. "I'd say one of Emma's caramel lattes but I'm watching my calories. How about a double . . . almond mocha."

"Yeah. Those are really low-cal," I laughed. "Never mind, you've got it!"

Carly tilted her head to the side, her lips pursed. "How is everything going for you? With the other gals, I see joy and freedom, but I'm not sensing that so much from you."

"I thought *I* was good at reading people!" I said, a bit annoyed. "What tipped you off?"

"It's your eyes, especially when people talk about their guilt being lifted."

Frustrated words flew from my mouth before I could contain them. "I can't. I can't forgive myself. I know God forgave me, but what I did was too terrible. What kind of mother would abandon her child when he needed her most? No, that's unforgivable. God is God. He can find forgiveness for me, but I cannot. It's just not that easy."

No matter how Carly tried to approach it, I was not open to her words. She left, promising to pray for me. I knew she would.

I stewed about it all weekend. If the meetings weren't being held in my coffee shop, I would have dropped out then and there. Why should I drag down everyone else?

They were all so happy and free, and now Carly knew my secret—that I was still in bondage as I'd been for thirty years. Nothing had changed. H.E.A.R.T. hadn't worked for me.

• • • • •

On Monday, Mariah came into the shop. She'd pulled her hair straight back, exposing her face. That should have been a good thing, yet those lovely features were hidden behind her giant horn-rimmed glasses. Poor, shy Mariah—totally lacking in confidence. And no wonder! Her mother had told her what to do all her life and now her boyfriend has taken over. If she doesn't obey him immediately, she's likely to receive a punch or a twisted arm. I've seen the wariness in her eyes, the bruises she tries to hide under those baggy plaid shirts.

"Hi, Liz," she said softly. "How're you doing?"

"Fine, Mariah. You got the day off? I don't usually see you until after your shift."

"Yeah, they've closed the plant for inventory. I signed a bid to work but was too low on the totem pole. I sure could have used the extra pay." Mariah's head dipped, as it did so often when she was embarrassed or frightened.

"You saving for something?"

"Yes, but don't tell anyone." She lowered her voice even though there was no one else in the shop. "I'm trying to put enough aside so I can get a place of my own, get away from my mother." Again the dipped head.

"You and she don't have the best relationship in the world, do you?" I motioned for her to sit down beside me on the barstools.

"I swear she hates me, always putting me down, always second-guessing every decision I make. According to her, I haven't done one thing right in my entire life." Mariah's shoulders slumped and tears formed in her eyes. She removed her glasses and searched in her bag for a tissue that wasn't there. She looked at me helplessly—I handed her a napkin.

"I'm so sorry, Mariah. You're both missing out on what could be a wonderful relationship—the mother-daughter bond." Inwardly, I was thinking about my own daughters, Jessica and Joy . . . both now living so far away. Jessica and I have that bond—as natural as you please, whereas Joy and I struggle to maintain one. It's not always easy.

"At least I don't know what I'm missing, never having experienced bonding with her." She shrugged her shoulders. "But, after all, I'm thirty-two years old. It's time I was on my own. I would have left long ago, but everything costs so much these days. Just getting an apartment, up front there's first and last month's rent, plus a cleaning deposit. That's more than a thousand dollars."

"Emma told me that her apartment runs $1100 per month," I said. "I don't know how young people do it."

"Emma's got a great tech job," Mariah said, without a hint of envy in her voice. "I'm a blue-collar worker. There's no way I could afford $1100 per month." She looked down at her feet. "Of course, her apartment is way too nice for me!"

"I wouldn't say that, Mariah, but I do agree Emma's place is beautiful."

"Yeah." She sounded wistful.

"Hey, you want something to drink?"

"Just a cup of regular decaf. Oh, and could you save room for cream?"

"With all the coffee drinks available, you always order the same boring thing. Is that your choice? Or do you order it because it costs less?"

"Probably a little of both." She shrugged.

"Today it's my treat, on the house! Order anything you want."

"Thanks, but the usual will be fine. And don't forget room for cream, please." Mariah was stuck in a rut.

"You sure?"

"Yes."

"All right then. But at least take a cookie for dunking." The mother in me just couldn't resist offering a little comfort food. "So what are your plans for your day off?" I asked.

Her tone took on a new urgency. "I came by especially to talk to you, Liz." She turned in her barstool to face me. "I know you raised daughters and have a lot of wisdom where girls are concerned."

"Thanks." It pleased me that Mariah felt that way. *What would it take for me to prove to Joy that I had wisdom?* "What did you want to talk about?"

"It's about my boyfriend, Rick."

"What about him?"

"If I do move out of my mother's house, I know he's going to want to move in with me." Mariah twisted her hair as she glanced back at the door. There was that look of sadness mixed with fear. *What would happen to her if they were living together?*

"How do you feel about that?"

"Not so good. I want to have some personal space for the first time in my life. Sharing expenses with someone would be nice, but Rick's not even working. I have a growing feeling that I'll end up paying all the expenses for both of us."

"That could very well happen."

"Well, we don't know for sure!" Mariah spoke defensively, putting those horrible glasses back on her sweet face. As tortuous as their relationship was, she still felt some need to defend Rick. "He could end up getting a really good job."

"Okay. Let's say he does. That would be a very good thing. However, cohabiting is not usually beneficial for the girl."

"What do you mean?"

Mariah had come to me for the truth and I needed to give it to her, gently. "Who do you think does most of the housework? Who do you think stays home from work or school to let the plumber in? Who do you think provides free entertainment at night? And who do you think gets left in the lurch when someone richer or prettier comes along?"

"It doesn't sound any different from marriage to me."

"At least a married person has security, Mariah. She has legal rights." I poured myself a cup of coffee and took a sip. "Speaking of marriage, you aren't thinking of marrying Rick, are you?"

"Not unless he changes quite a bit. Sometimes he's mean to me."

I wanted to say I know.

She gently caressed her forearm where I'd earlier noticed a bruise. "But then again, things could be different if we were living together and learning how to get along. They say living together can be good preparation for marriage."

"Yes, I've heard that argument. But I've also heard that people who live together before marriage have a much higher divorce rate than those who don't. So compatible or not, cohabiting is frequently not a good thing."

Mariah sighed and dropped her head.

"What if you get pregnant with Rick? Do you think he'd stay with you and be a father to the child?"

"No." She shook her head slowly, lowering her eyes. "He's already said he doesn't want children. I freaked out when he said that, and told him I'd never get another abortion."

"What'd he say to that?"

"He just stomped out the door."

Taking Mariah's hands in mine, I asked, "Honey, why are you with this man?"

Mariah once again removed her glasses, hung her head, and whispered, so quietly I could scarcely hear, "Oh, he's not so bad. I've known worse. You see, I seem to attract men who just drag me down farther and farther until I don't even know what I want anymore."

Then, mustering all her strength, Mariah sat up straight and spoke forcefully. "I *do* know I want to leave home. I know I want to grow up. I want to be a big girl and make my own decisions." Her strength disappearing as quickly as it had come, she dissolved in tears. "But I don't know how."

And wouldn't you just know—right then when I wanted to draw her close and speak motherly assurances to her—the door opened and some customers walked in.

Mariah drew herself up, blew her nose, gave me a nod, and left with her coffee, whispering, "I'll see you on Wednesday."

Yes, I will see you on Wednesday and on any day that you need my help, sweet Mariah.

Chapter Five

Emma's Transformation

Before noon on Wednesday, my heart began to flutter with excitement. I prepared to welcome the group with renewed vigor, understanding that although H.E.A.R.T. hadn't helped me, this was not about me. It was about them, women like Mariah, Emma, and Susan, who'd suffered through abortion and its aftermath. They needed reassurance; they needed love and guidance. They needed Carly and Annie. And they needed me, too.

So what if I still carried around a boatload of guilt? That was the price I'd always pay for my actions. But there was hope for these women and I wanted to be part of restoring it to them.

Wanting tonight to be special, I decorated the shop with balloons and festive paper streamers from the party store across the street. I put out some scones and made two kinds of flavored coffee, Kahlua Crème and Chocolate Velvet.

I waited eagerly for Mariah to come, wondering if there had been any new developments since Monday. I hoped she would share her story tonight; and if not Mariah, then who?

Personally, I no longer had any desire to talk about myself and my problems.

Carly was the first to arrive. "So, Liz, are you going to tell your story tonight?"

"No," I said. "Mariah came in this week and I'm hoping she'll feel like telling hers. I think it would be good for her."

"And I think it would be good for you to share yours," Carly said, looking squarely at me.

"Another time," I said coolly, hoping she'd get the message and wouldn't press.

"Okay," Carly said. "Whatever." She winked at me and smiled.

Before I could respond, Emma breezed in. "Carly, can I tell my story tonight? I've been thinking about what Annie shared all week! I want to go next."

Carly looked at me. We both looked at the bubbly twenty-two-year-old, so eager to share, and said in unison, "Sure!"

"Groovy," Emma winked, looking around the shop. "Wow, Liz, everything looks so festive. And doesn't the coffee smell good? I may develop a new favorite."

The rest all came in at once. It was obvious to me that Mariah was in no state to share her story anyway. I wondered if there had been another fight with Rick, some reason to make her look so sad and withdrawn. Taking her aside, I asked, "Mariah, you all right?"

"No. Rick and I had a bad fight last night. I told him my plans to get a place of my own. He thought it was great until I told him I intended to live by myself. Then he hit the roof and threatened to tell my mother what I was planning to do."

"Is it so bad that your mother knows?"

"Liz, you just don't understand. You would never understand someone like my mother." Mariah's glasses began to fog up and I knew that tears were close.

"Why not, Mariah? She's a woman, isn't she?"

"She's not at all like you—I wish she were. I'd love to have you for a mother."

How come Mariah thinks I'm so wonderful and my own Joy hardly gives me the time of day? Mariah simply doesn't understand what an unfit mother I am.

"Come see me this week, whenever you can make it. I'm sure we can figure out what to do with Rick if we put our heads together."

"Thanks, Liz. I'll call you."

With a smile, I turned to the rest of the group. "Hey, everybody, tonight we have the pleasure of hearing from Emma. So, if you haven't already done so, please help yourself to the coffee and scones. Then Emma can have the floor."

• • • • •

"Where to begin?" Emma giggled, looking around the room. "I was so inspired by Annie's story last week that I couldn't wait to get back and take my turn. Now I'm thinking maybe I should've waited."

Carly smiled. "I always feel that way when I get up in front of people. Just start anywhere and before you know it, you'll be making sense."

"I've never made sense in my life," Emma joked. "Why should I start now? But—okay, here goes. And I really hope you *can* make sense out of this. Sometimes I feel like we speak different languages." She looked directly at me and Annie.

"What do you mean?" I asked.

"Well," Emma said, "sometimes listening to you and Annie talk is like reading a history book. Your memories are so different from mine. You talk about things that happened before I was born, things I don't know anything about."

"That's nothing," Annie said. "You talk about things that happen today that we don't know about—like rap music, grunge, MP3 players."

"Don't forget BlackBerries," I said.

"Yeah, blackberries." Annie raised her hands heavenward. "Are they related to raspberries and loganberries, or are they more like a blackcap?"

"What about hook-ups and booty calls and friends with benefits?" Carly looked at me and Annie. "I'll bet you don't know what they are either."

"Should we?"

"All right, we're even," said Emma, throwing up her hands in mock disgust. "For good or for bad, we've all been touched by the culture we grew up in. Let's hope you can understand where I'm coming from."

Emma settled comfortably in her chair and, with a smile at each of us, began to tell us her story.

• • • • •

My folks are both professional people and have worked at their careers all my life. Mom is a psychiatrist in a family counseling practice and Dad is a sociology professor at Portland State University. I spent much of my growing up years at the university attending concerts and lectures, things that Dad thought would have a good influence on me.

I'm afraid that I was influenced even more by the cultural styles and attitudes of the students. Long before my middle-school classmates began to wear Gothic or grunge, I picked up on those trends from a group of PSU students. I was first in my class to wear black fingernail polish and spiky hair.

For entertainment I would hide in the stalls of the university bathrooms and eavesdrop on students talking about their boyfriends and what they did on their dates. Then I would go back to middle school and tell my classmates.

At first we were shocked and put off. But then, we recognized that these things were being talked about all the time—we just hadn't been tuned in to the clues on MTV and in the movies. We began to notice explicit sexual messages in commercials, even shampoo commercials. "You gotta have it. You gotta want it."

We began to want it—at least to want to know more about it. Sex became a topic of intense interest to us. One afternoon, we gathered at my house to watch an Oprah exposé involving young teens in a Midwestern town performing sexual acts on one another. What tipped off authorities to the teen orgies was an unusually high rate of syphilis in that town, especially in upscale neighborhoods where kids came home to empty houses.

I won't shock you with details. It's enough to say that these kids were doing everything imaginable to one another. I mean everything.

Oprah interviewed some of them and their mothers and challenged them to consider how they were hurting themselves, both physically and emotionally, with these kinds of practices. They showed no sign of remorse—and they seemed to see no reason to quit.

In fact, neither did we. We decided to check it out, thinking that anything Midwestern kids could do, we could do better in Portland. Assembling a mixed group of our own, we attempted each and every weird thing they were doing. If we knew about it, we did it. By the time I was a freshman, there was little I didn't know about the mechanics of sex.

One Friday afternoon Mr. Henderson, our health teacher, announced we were going to have a guest speaker on Monday talking about sex—and abstinence. Abstinence! The whole class erupted in laughter.

My friends and I had a weekend of partying planned, so I didn't give much thought to this guest speaker.

• • • • •

"Wait just a doggone minute there, missy," Annie interjected. "You were a freshman in high school?"

"Just barely," Emma answered. "Pretty lame, huh!"

"In my day, we thought that making out in the back of the old Chevy was living on the edge."

"Well, it was—then. Wasn't it?" said Emma. "I mean think about it, Annie. You could get just as pregnant in the back of that old Chevy—and there wasn't any way out, like emergency contraception and easy access to abortion."

"We could get abortions," Annie grimaced, remembering her own frightening experience: the darkened room, the painful scraping, and the smell of blood.

"Sure, but abortions weren't as easy to get as they are now."

Annie nodded. "You're right, Emma. Today the consequences don't seem as daunting. People are more accepting of unplanned pregnancy in the first place."

"And yet," added Susan. "I worry about my kids constantly. They don't see the risks involved—not only of pregnancy, but also of sexually-transmitted diseases, even AIDS."

I nodded. "A friend of my daughter Jessica will never have children because of a disease—Chlamydia, I think it's called—that she picked up sometime during her teens."

"Then there's the rise in cervical cancer resulting from HPV," said Carly.

"These things all matter to me now. However, as a teen, I thought I was invincible." Emma cleared her throat and continued her story.

• • • • •

Anyway, on Monday afternoon, a bunch of us walked toward health class expecting to see some sour middle-aged spinster or some preachy old man ready to talk to us about our sex lives. We had real attitudes back then, coming into the classroom with smart ass remarks.

Up front was this tall, gorgeous woman that Mr. Henderson introduced as Kelly, a representative of the Pregnancy Resource Centers of Portland. She was really confident, spoke with authority, and the best part was that she seemed to care about what happened to us.

• • • • •

"I know Kelly," interjected Annie, excitedly. "She's terrific! She came to your class? She was one of the best abstinence speakers we ever had at PRC."

Emma smiled. "I thought you'd know her. It is a small world, isn't it, Miss Annie? Yes, Kelly came."

• • • • •

She came, she saw, she conquered—the boys first and then the girls.

We weren't prepared for someone like Kelly. She told us the truth, about herself, her sexual history before marriage, and how it had affected her whole life. She told about the baby she had and how she'd struggled as a single parent until she later married.

Kelly also told us the truth about our own sex lives. She knew all about our secret activities under the bleachers during games and the things we did after school at home. When some claimed they were still virgins since they didn't actually have sexual intercourse—even though they did everything else—she called their bluff. And she showed us pictures, really gross pictures, of body parts infected with sexually transmitted diseases.

She told us about secondary virginity and challenged us to refrain from sex from that point forward, to stop all sexual activity until our wedding day. Several of my friends made a commitment that very afternoon and stuck to their decision. Not me.

If anything, I wanted to prove Kelly wrong. I wanted to prove that I was different, that her story may be true for her, but not for me. I wanted to continue life as I knew it because, frankly, I liked sex. It felt good, and I believed I wielded a certain kind of power over the boys who competed to be with me. I learned I could approach a group of guys and, with a simple facial expression or low throaty sound, have them panting after me like puppy dogs.

• • • • •

"Emma. If you'd been my daughter, I'd have had you over my knee so fast!" I said.

"I'd have locked you up," Susan added. "If Melissa ever did such things, I'd go find me one of those chastity belts you read about in medieval history."

"I'm sure my parents would have done the same thing if they'd known. But they were clueless, so focused on their careers." Emma sighed and went on with the rest of her story.

• • • • •

Years later, I came to realize I was delusional. I wasn't the one with the power—I was the one giving up the power. I was the pawn. The boys got whatever they wanted and I literally gave myself away bit by bit.

By the time I was a junior in high school, many boys were afraid to go out with me because word had gotten around that I had an STD. The truth is I suspected I did—though I'd been careful not to tell anyone.

I'd purposely *not* gone to the school health clinic because I didn't want my classmates to suspect anything, and I'd purposely *not* gone to my family doctor because I didn't want my parents to find out. One day, sensing that something was definitely wrong with me, I skipped school and visited the County Health Department where I learned that millions of teens are infected with an STD each year. I learned I was one of them and will continue to battle outbreaks of genital herpes for the rest of my life. It's not fun.

When I told my parents, they were devastated, shocked, angry, mortified. Mother, the psychiatrist, tried to analyze where she and Dad had gone wrong. Dad, the sociology professor, cited statistics for these kinds of things. They were grieved, disappointed, and disillusioned—how could I have done this to them?

It was bad—but nothing like when they discovered I was also pregnant. Let's just say feathers flew. Mother descended like a mythical harpy upon the head of her wayward daughter. Dad, like a wounded eagle, flew in a rage to pluck out the eyes of my boyfriend. Nothing "professional" about them now—they were parents!

Frankly, it thrilled me to see them so angry. I felt very important, very significant. Maybe they loved me after all.

We held family discussions. We wept together—held hands. We planned our next move. I didn't particularly care what the move would be, so long as we did it together, as a family. Our decision was to abort.

I was too young to have a baby, unmarried, and certainly not able to care for a child of my own. My mother had a career and no intentions of complicating her life with another baby. Dad didn't say much but he seemed relieved with the decision. One less thing to think about.

I had the abortion on Friday and by Monday was well enough to go back to school. However, I was so depressed that Mother allowed me to stay home an extra day. Funny thing, though—she stayed home, too. Amazing!

She sat on the end of my bed, legs crossed, looking more like one of my girlfriends than my mom. She asked me how I felt, wondered if she could help. She apologized for not having been home more, for giving me way too much freedom before I could handle it. Mother cried about her errors in judgment, saying she should have listened to her heart more than her head.

Then, peering out from behind her bangs, she asked if I'd like to hear a story. Nodding, I lay my head back on the pillow and closed my eyes, trying not to fall asleep. Not a problem. In seconds I was wide awake, spellbound by her tale.

It was a story about us, her and me, and how we had begun our lives together. I was conceived when she and Dad were dating and they were both still in college. Both very career-minded, they hadn't planned on marriage; yet when I came along, they did the "right thing."

Mom was quick to explain herself. "Oh, we've never regretted it, Emma. We have a good marriage and we love you dearly. It's just that some people are more nurturing than others, and neither Dad nor I score very high in that category. If you know what I mean."

Of course, I know what you mean. Haven't I experienced it all these years? Haven't I wished that you could take a turn as room mother or come along on a field trip—at least once? Haven't I longed to come home from school to a plate of cookies and a listening ear?

"And now I realize," Mom continued, "that whether or not a person is a born nurturer, she still owes it to her child, the child she has chosen to bring into the world, to spend time with her, to be there for her. I wasn't there for you, Emma, and that is a large part of why we're sitting here today, on your bed, fighting depression."

I hung my head, tears flowing freely down my cheeks. Mother took my face in her hands and kissed it. "I'm so very sorry, Emma. Can you forgive me for being a bad mother?"

I looked at her. "You may think you were a bad mother. But I'm no mother at all. I have a hole inside me, an empty hole where a baby was, my baby. I didn't even fight for her. I didn't even do the 'right thing' like you and Dad did. What does that make me?"

"It makes you very young, Emma; and, for you, this was the 'right thing.'"

"I don't think so. Before the abortion, I looked at the ultrasound screen; I saw a baby there. It had eyes and ears, toes and fingers, and almost seemed to be waving at me. At that point, I wanted to keep my baby, but I said nothing. I just let it happen. How can I live with that?"

"I didn't know, Emma. I always heard that it's only a blob of tissue. Are you sure you saw those things? Eyes and ears, fingers, waving?"

"Positive." And then I cried some more. We both cried, the realization setting in that not only had we aborted my baby but my mother's grandchild as well. Mom stretched out on my bed, holding me in her arms, and we fell asleep, dead to the world. By the time Dad got home from work, he found two different women, a mother and daughter who had found each other even in the rubble of death.

Our lives changed immediately. Mom rearranged her schedule so that she was always home by 2:30 in the afternoon. She began to explore domestic pursuits, discovering to her surprise that she enjoyed baking bread and creating soups and slow-cooked meals in the crock pot. We ate in more, enjoying leisurely talks around the dinner table.

That's when I discovered that I really liked my dad. He understood life in the twenty-first century and could explain the "forces that drive cultures." He helped me understand why my generation looks at life differently from previous generations and he helped me understand why I struggled so much in high school.

One night Dad said to me, "Emma, my big mistake where you're concerned is that I had this knowledge but failed to apply it to my own family. It was strictly academic for me, when what I needed to do was to take it personally."

When I asked him what he meant by that, he said, "I should have protected you from the filth on TV and movies; but, instead, I was . . . writing scholarly articles."

• • • • •

Emma cleared her throat and looked at us, sitting on the edge of our chairs, tears in our eyes. "Although much of what Dad said about culture was over my head, I now recognize that, as a group, my peers and I really are different from you guys. We're more team-oriented whereas your generation values individual effort. Your generation prizes absolutes, but my generation appreciates diversity and doing what is right in our own eyes."

"Which begs the question 'Who's right?'" I asked. "I mean if everyone is doing what's right in their own eyes, how does anyone know who, or what, is right? There's no universal standard."

Annie got up to refill her coffee mug. "You're speaking my language . . . that's the way I see things, too. We do have a gap here in the way we look at things, a real generation gap. But at the pregnancy center, we're being trained to see things through the young peoples' eyes in order to be able to communicate with them. You can't guide someone until you know where she's coming from."

"I don't know where my own kids are coming from half the time," Susan added. "They're my flesh and blood, and yet some of their ideas seem to come from Mars."

"So back to my question. Who, and what, is right?" I asked.

"I don't know who's right, Liz, or if there even is a right way," said Emma, looking around the room at us. "I just see that this is how things are."

Annie spoke up. "I've noticed that very way of thinking among the clients who come into the pregnancy center. I tell them about Jesus who, for me, is the absolute and only way to God. They look at me, smile, and nod in agreement. Then later I learn that they also are sympathetic to the claims of the Wiccans or the Buddhists."

"How do you evangelize a generation like that? And how do I disciple my own children?" Susan raised her arms to heaven in exasperation.

"You just have to continue to trust that God's mercy is everlasting and that his truth endures to all generations, just like the scriptures say," Annie concluded.

"That's good, Annie," I added. "And something else just occurred to me. God still speaks to individuals—our Emma is a good case in point. She's very much a child of her generation and yet the Lord spoke to her heart. She may be 'postmodern' and I may be an aging 'baby boomer,' but we both have been made new in Christ—and the same is true for believers through the centuries. His truth does endure to all generations."

"Gosh, does that mean God knows what he's doing?" Annie asked with a grin. "It's a good thing he's in control of things, because if it were left up to us humans, we'd be in deep doo-doo."

"Deep doo-doo? Was that one of your Haight-Ashbury expressions, Annie, along with *groovy* and *make love, not war*?" Emma laughed.

With a smirk, Annie nodded to Emma, "Just continue with your story."

• • • • •

As Dad and Mom and I began to reform ourselves as a family, I began to change as a human being. Leaving behind the grunge attire was easy. Leaving behind my sexual reputation was another thing. People had come to see me in a certain light and weren't able to view me any other way. I was largely seen as a whore.

The girls shunned me; the boys steered clear of me—they'd already found other "true loves." Never was anyone so glad to graduate from high school. I left the building, with all its painful associations, without a backward glance.

The summer between high school and college was my time to gain some perspective. I could stay inside my safe little world, peopled now with me, my mom, and dad. Or I could reach out and make some new friends.

Mom thought I should make some new friends. "Emma, don't hang around the house all day long. You need to find some nice young people who will make you laugh again."

"I don't know any nice young people," I answered. "Why would nice young people want to be around me after the way I've been?" I didn't blame them. When I'd been the go-to girl, I hadn't always been kind to others—in fact, I'd been pretty nasty.

"Honey, you're being way too hard on yourself. Okay, you made some poor choices in the past. But that's behind you. You have a chance to start over, so let's consider why people, nice people, would want to be around you."

"I'm listening."

I used to kid Mom about putting on her psychiatrist's hat when she was trying to understand me or my behavior. Here she was doing it again. "Emma, let's pretend someone is seeing you for the first time. What would they see?" Mom looked at me critically, her head tilted to one side. "First off, you're pretty. You have a nice look about you—friendly."

"Now that the black fingernail polish and spiky purple hair are gone?" That was one of the first changes I made once our family began to be a family.

"Well, yes, that did detract from your overall appearance."

"Why did you let me go out of the house like that anyway?" I laughed, remembering how much Mom and Dad hated the way I looked.

"Could I have stopped you, Emma? You can be one stubborn young woman! But even that can be a plus and a real reason for someone to appreciate you."

"How's that?" I thought, *Leave it to my mother to find something positive in everything.*

"Your stubbornness, used in the right way, can make you a real champion for good things in life."

"Like what?"

"Like whatever," Mom said. "Whatever you choose to champion, whomever you choose to befriend. You're tenacious and you will accomplish whatever you set out to do."

"So I'm pretty and I'm tenacious. What else am I?" Actually, I was gaining courage the longer Mom talked. Maybe I'd begin to believe her.

"You're bright. Before you got off track in middle school, there was no stopping you in class. You read more books than anyone in fifth grade and wrote wonderful poems and songs. I miss your poems.

"And another thing—you're a leader. Remember in third grade when the little Cambodian girl came to your school? She spoke no English but you took her under your wing and faithfully helped integrate her into your class. Your other friends accepted her simply because you made her your friend. You've always been a leader and friendships have always been important to you, Emma."

I decided Mom was right—I needed friends. But where would I find them? Since I hadn't been able to get work for the summer, Dad suggested I come down to PSU with him every day and volunteer in the sociology department. *Why not?*

The people in Dad's department were friendly and found lots for me to do. I made copies, ran errands, did computer work, filed papers.

One day, delivering some papers to another office, I saw a familiar face from the past. It was Kelly, the abstinence speaker from the pregnancy center. I did a double-take when I saw how she was dressed.

Looking like a co-ed herself, Kelly was wearing spandex shorts and a T-shirt, carrying a bicycle helmet, and toting a large notebook under her arm.

If she'd been dressed professionally, I might not have had the nerve to say anything. Instead, "Hey, Kelly!" I called.

She stopped, turned around, and stared at me blankly.

"I know you don't remember me, but I sat through two of your abstinence presentations when I was a student at Southridge High School."

"Yeah?" She cocked her head to the side. "And what did you think?" Kelly's abstinence message usually evoked two responses. There were students who'd risk being late to their next class just so they could talk to her and ask questions . . . and there were others who tuned her out and avoided any contact with her at all.

"I thought it was a waste of time," I admitted, dropping my eyes from her gaze.

"So, where are you at now?" Kelly asked, continuing to look directly at me.

"I've changed my mind. And I want to thank you for doing what you do. Don't stop, no matter what kids like me think at the time."

"What's your name?" Kelly asked, smiling calmly at me.

"Emma Matthews. I was in Mr. Henderson's freshman health class and in Mrs. Harper's social science class."

"Your face looks familiar—but weren't you one of the grunge group? Spiked hair? Black fingernail polish?"

"Yeah," I confessed. "That was me. I had a real attitude at the time. Plus I was fooling around and didn't like your saying things that might mess with my life."

"But I take it you've moved on," Kelly said kindly. It was as much a question as a statement.

"Yes. I had a baby, too." I felt I needed to tell her . . . to face the reality of what I'd done . . . to make a kind of confession to her.

"You did?"

"But, unlike you, I didn't keep it. I had an abortion," I confessed.

Kelly's smile evaporated. She bowed her head, lips curving downward, her eyes saddened. "I'm sorry, Emma. How are you handling that?"

"It was awful. It's still awful. But I'm forcing myself to press on. The one good thing that has come out of it is that my parents and I have grown closer."

Kelly told me about a post-abortion recovery group but I wasn't ready for anything like that yet. She also told me about a group of young people who met near the campus at noon every day to pray and encourage one another. *That might be good,* I thought.

"Call Renee Day—here's her number. She's a neat gal, about your age." Kelly gave me a hug. "Here's my number, too, in case you want to talk." She looked at her watch. "Oops, I've gotta go. I'm late to class. Take care, Emma."

As Kelly raced off, I pondered the coincidence of running into her, of all people, and getting a lead on some possible new friends . . . nice new friends.

Kelly had said that these kids get together to pray and encourage one another. They were probably Christians. I wondered what they'd think of me if they knew about my past. *Oh, I don't care. This is my chance to meet some new people, people my own age, and they certainly couldn't treat me any worse than my own crowd did.*

That night, I called Renee and arranged to meet her the following morning in the PSU cafeteria. I found her alone at a table in the corner, pouring over piles of sheet music. A music major, she was preparing for a recital the following weekend.

"Do you sing?" she asked me, her large brown eyes catching mine.

"No," I responded, thinking, *My choice of music would probably shock her and her nice Christian friends.*

"Play anything?" She continued shuffling her sheet music.

"Cards," I answered, deadpan. "Solitaire, hearts, gin rummy."

Renee stopped with the music, looked up at me, and broke into an enormous grin. "Can you file?"

"That's all I seem to do these days—in the sociology department."

"Then help me, will you? I have this enormous pile of music that needs to be filed alphabetically. We can visit while we work." Dividing the music in two, we each took a stack and began to sort.

"Our friend Kelly told me about the group you belong to that meets daily to encourage one another," I said. "I'm interested in knowing more about it and wonder if you'd fill me in."

"Sure. Actually, we meet in about twenty minutes. You want to come with me today? I'll introduce you around to the others.

I owe you that much for the filing." Renee looked at me and said, "You look vaguely familiar. Do you go to PSU?"

"No," I said. "My dad's on staff here and I'm just helping out through the summer until I start college in the fall."

"Where're you going?"

"University of Oregon," I said. "In Eugene."

"Majoring in what?"

"Liberal Arts. I don't know yet what I want to do."

"That's scary. I've always known what I wanted to do. Music, music, music! My whole family's musical. My sister took ballet for years, my brother plays the drums, my dad sings and acts, and my mother sings, plays the piano, and teaches music at Southridge High School."

"Renee Day! Your mother is Mrs. Day?" I nearly shouted.

"Yes, you know her?"

"Know her? She was one of the few teachers I liked in high school. I took music thinking it would be an easy credit, something I could take and fake. But I was wrong. Your mother made the class interesting and challenging. She picked out music that touched my heart; and in those days, nothing touched my heart."

"What's your name again?" Renee asked. "I'll have to tell mother I met you."

I couldn't help hoping that Renee would forget to tell her mother about me. What if Mrs. Day told her what I was like in high school, a trampy little girl with a foul mouth and no morals.

"Oh, she won't remember me," I answered, looking down. "I didn't contribute much to the class, but I did like the music, and I did enjoy performing."

"Well, that explains why you look familiar. I didn't go to Southridge," explained Renee, "but I often attended Mom's concerts. I must have seen you there."

"Maybe. Although I've changed quite a bit since those days."

"Haven't we all?" Renee smiled. "Well, look at this," she said, staring at the two finished piles of music, "I never dreamed we'd get this sorting done. Thanks. Now let's get going or we'll be late for the meeting."

Crossing the Park Blocks, we passed the Portland Art Museum and the statue of Teddy Roosevelt astride his big bronze horse. We walked to a large brick apartment house where Renee rang the buzzer for apartment number 122 and announced us. I heard a click and glanced at the front door just as two girls were coming out.

"Hi, Renee. Go on in, the gang is mostly there. We're just running to Safeway for some chips and salsa." Looking at me as she passed, the shorter one said, "Hi! We'll be right back."

"That was Susie. And the girl with her was Martha," explained Renee. "They're good friends, go everywhere together. Lots of fun."

"Are they musical, too?" I asked.

Rene paused to think. "No. They're more into languages, romance languages, I think. They've talked about going on the study-abroad program in Perugia when they're juniors."

"Perugia—that's in Italy, isn't it?"

"Yes, you've heard of it?"

"My mom studied there when she was a junior in college. Absolutely loved it and still meets with some of her old classmates from that year." *Mom's lucky,* I thought, *to have friendships that are solid and have stood the test of time. Maybe someday I will, too.*

As we entered the building I noticed that the halls were dark and long. Every now and then there'd be a light bulb outside a door marking the entrance to someone's sanctuary. At the end of the hall, the door opened at apartment number 122.

Half a dozen people had already assembled. Adding Renee and me and Susie and Martha, the tiny living room would be packed. And yet people kept coming—two boys, three more girls, another girl, and a boy. We were seventeen in all, thigh-to-thigh on the couch, shoulder-to-shoulder on the floor.

I was impressed by everyone's genuine concern for one another, the overall tone of respect in the room. There was no coarseness or rude joking, just a general sense of joy and good cheer, encouragement and hope. I felt happy being there among them. No one made a big deal about my presence; they just welcomed me without question. Then they started to pray.

They prayed about their summer jobs and the people they worked with. They prayed about their classes, their finances, and their living accommodations for the coming year. They prayed for their professors. They prayed for one another, and they prayed for me. I just listened, not knowing how to pray. Then, all too soon, the hour was over and Renee and I were walking out the door.

"Mind if we join you?" Susie asked as she and Martha followed us out.

I wondered about the study-abroad program and asked Susie and Martha about their plans for Perugia. In the process, I discovered that both of them were planning to attend the University of Oregon in the fall and would study Italian.

"I'm going to the U of O, too," I told them. "I'll probably see you there."

"Have you got your dorm assignment yet?" Susie asked. "Martha and I are rooming together in Carson Hall."

"Me, too! My mother roomed in Carson Hall eons ago. She said I'd like being so close to everything."

"It is close to everything, plus it's got all that history and tradition—ghosts of former coeds lurking around the halls," laughed Martha. "Are you going to join the Christian Club on campus?"

"I didn't even know there was one," I confessed. "Are you?"

"For sure!" said Susie.

"Then I will, too." There was something about Susie and Martha that made me want to do whatever they did. Especially Susie. From her tailored shirt and classy cardigan to her tussled hair, close-cropped and stylish, she radiated joy, confidence, spunk. Nothing phony about her, not even make up!

• • • • •

That night at dinner, Mom noticed I was different. "How was your meeting today? You seem happy, more at peace."

"Why do you say that?" I asked.

"Well, from the moment you got home, you've been humming. You set the table without being asked, filled our glasses, wiped off the counter, actually escorted Dad to dinner instead of yelling. You just seem—different."

"I like these kids, Mom. They're a little churchy, but they're kind and honest and they welcomed me. I didn't feel like an outcast among them at all."

Mom put her arm around me. "You've had a pretty tough time the past couple of years, haven't you. I'm glad you have found some new friends."

And that was that! Soon these new friends became my good friends. And before I knew it, they'd introduced me to their best friend, Jesus, who became my best friend forever.

Jesus helped me all through college, including my unforgettable year in Perugia with Susie and Martha. By the time we left Italy to return home, we were all three fluent in Italian and madly in love with the country and its people.

• • • • •

"Which explains your Tuscan apartment!" said Mariah.

"Yes, I studied everything Italian, including Tuscan colors and interior design, and brought them home to my apartment. Every month or so, Susie and Martha come over and we have a big spaghetti feed with 'insalata verde e pane fresco.'"

"That's salad and bread, right?" chuckled Annie. "I spent some time in Italy, too—Little Italy, San Francisco, USA."

"You learned Italian very well." Emma smiled at Annie. "Bravo."

"Grazie, Cara." Annie rolled her eyes at the rest of us, showing off her limited vocabulary.

"Prego," Emma responded.

"All right. All right. How about a little English for the rest of us," I squawked. "I could show off, too, with my extensive Italian vocabulary. Let's see, I've spent time in a Portland café and have learned to say cappucino . . . espresso . . . biscotti . . ."

Laughing, Carly held up her hand and looked at Emma. "All kidding aside, Emma, it sounds like you have put your abortion in the past and are moving ahead. You're fortunate that you were able to deal with it at a young age rather than have it dominate your life for ten or even twenty years like many women of previous generations."

Emma paused, her head leaning to the side as if in thought. "I wonder if that isn't one good thing about my generation. Because we aren't as likely to embrace absolutes, we're possibly not so hard on ourselves or others."

"Hmmm, I'd have to think about that one," I said. "Are you saying that it's good to stand for nothing, so that when you fall, it's not that big of a deal?"

Emma shrugged her shoulders. "I'm just saying that when we recognize we've made a mistake, we admit it and move on. I know I made a mistake, a huge one. But now, rather than throw my life away as a lost cause, I want to make something good happen out of that mistake."

"What do you want to do, Emma?" asked Mariah shyly. Though she was ten years older, Mariah had begun to look to Emma for answers.

"I don't know. But I've heard about an organization known as Feminists for Life that has branches on college campuses. They're feminists but they're also pro-life, speaking openly about how bad abortion has been for women. I want to support organizations like that. I also want to be part of the Silent No More campaign."

"What's that?"

"It's a big deal, Mariah. Hundreds of thousands of women who've had abortions are speaking out publicly, telling their stories to anyone who will listen." Emma continued. "Carly has told us about the many post-abortive women who cower in fear of being 'found out.' It seems to me we have a choice. We can cower in fear or we can boldly stand against what has hurt us so much."

"Emma's right," said Carly, looking at the rest of us. "Hanging our heads in shame is not the answer. We've been forgiven and set free—for a purpose. I believe that purpose is to spare others the sorrow we've experienced, and to save the babies whose lives hang in the balance. In the process, we glorify God by acknowledging that human life, which he created in his image, is sacred."

Echoes of agreement sounded around the tables. Then, because it was late and we were all tired, we stood to leave. Quietly, and solemnly, we hugged one another. Was it my imagination or did something seem different tonight? Maybe we were experiencing a new sense of mission, an urgency to expose the wrongs we had experienced.

• • • • •

On Thursday morning, right after I opened the shop, Carly walked in. "Liz, I have to talk to you."

"About Emma? Isn't she a firecracker? Maybe there's hope for our world yet."

"No. Not about Emma," Carly said.

She has this look in her eyes. What does she want? "Carly, I do *not* plan to tell my story next week. I may *never* tell my story."

Sliding her arm through mine, Carly said, "Liz, I'm not here to talk about that. You can tell your story when you're ready. I need to talk to you about something else."

"What?" I finished wiping down the counter and put the morning paper out for my customers to read. "You want some coffee first?"

"No thanks," she said. "Do you remember when I told my story? Right in the middle, I realized I had some unfinished business."

"You mean Eric?"

"Yes," Carly said. Looking me straight in the eye, she continued. "I asked the group to hold me accountable. Pretty soon, someone, probably Emma, is going to want to know what I've done to find out what happened to him."

"You're right. She mentioned it to me a week or two ago."

"Liz, I'm not sure what to do." She pulled up a chair and sat down.

I grabbed a cup of coffee and sat down with her. "I guess you could hire a detective. But wouldn't it be easier to ask some of your Seattle friends?"

"I really don't want them involved."

"How about your brother, Kurt? Could he do some checking for you?"

"He'd probably wonder why I'm digging up the past, especially that part. Besides he might let it slip to Joe, and I'm not sure I want him to know. Remembering what a wreck I was following my relationship with Eric, he'd naturally want me to stay far away from him."

"Then maybe you should." The more I'd thought about Carly making any kind of a connection with Eric, the more uneasy I felt. What good could come of it?

"Liz, I feel duty bound to find out what happened to Eric. He could still be in a hospital, with no one looking out for his best interests. If I find him, I don't know what I could do for him. I just want to know—and help if I can."

"I think these are your options, Carly—a detective, your friends, or your brother."

Carly nodded at me, then suggested the obvious. "What about the phone book?"

"Well, duh!" I felt foolish that I hadn't even thought of the phone book.

Carly continued. "I'll start there then. Can't you also find people through the Internet?"

"See, you don't need me, Carly. You're the one with all the ideas."

"I may have ideas," Carly said, raising her eyebrows, "but I'm scared to death. And I do need you. In fact I came today to ask if you'd help me close this chapter of my life, once and for all."

"Why me, Carly? You don't know me, not really."

"No, I don't. But I do know Annie, and she thinks the world of you. She said that in the years she's known you, you've proven to be wise and caring . . . you tell the truth, and you can be tough as nails, if need be. I need someone strong, Liz. I need you to help me."

It was reassuring that Annie had said these things about me. Ever since I'd heard of her abortion, I'd wondered about our relationship. Why hadn't she told me? *Maybe she doesn't value my friendship as much as I value hers*? But she'd told Carly that

I was someone worth knowing. "Then count me in. What can I do?"

Carly said, "Come with me to Seattle and help me poke around—just for the day. I'll research the phone book and Internet ahead of time, and I'll phone City Hall for any public information they may have. Then if you'd drive up with me on a Sunday, we could do the legwork. I chose Sunday so you wouldn't have to close the shop."

"Okay. Let's do it. When do you want to go, this Sunday?"

"Next. Joe's preaching this week and I need time to find a substitute for my Sunday school class."

As Carly left, I shook my head. *First Mariah and now Carly—two young women who think I have something to offer. Amazing!*

• • • • •

Mariah checked in on Friday. She and Rick were still arguing over her future plans and the apartment he had hoped to share with her. I was beginning to dislike that man more intensely every day!

Would Mariah ever explain why she didn't want her mother to know she was moving out? Every time I tried to broach the subject, she'd deftly side-step it—like one who's learned to avoid anything unpleasant.

When she left that day, I knew little more than I did last week. Yet, I liked the fact that she came and was learning to trust me.

• • • • •

The following Monday afternoon, Susan came into the shop. She rarely dropped in, so this was a surprise. I quickly served up her decaf vanilla latte. When she dropped her eyes to her coffee, I couldn't help noticing that, for someone who is normally so "put together," she was a sight—messy hair, smeared eye makeup, wrinkled top. She looked like she just got out of bed or, worse, had never gone to bed.

"Liz, I wanted to talk with you before Wednesday night. Would you be offended if I dropped out of the group?"

"Why do you want to drop out of the group?" I asked. "What's going on?"

"Well, look at me, Liz. I'm a mess, and my life's a mess, too. I just don't feel like sharing my story, and there is just you, Mariah, and me left."

"Susan, can you tell me what's wrong? Is it something temporary, or is this a long-term problem?"

"It's long-term, Liz," she said, tears running down her cheeks. Grabbing a napkin, she rubbed her eyes and blew her nose. "Keeping my family together is like trying to prop up a house of cards. We do okay until any breeze of adversity passes our way. Then we all fall apart. First it was Melissa, now it's Corey."

"What's wrong with Corey?"

"You know what? I can't talk about it now." She shook her head slowly side to side. "I'm just too tired, too tired of the whole thing. If I can hold on until he moves out, I think I'll be okay."

The bell on the front door jingled and two suits walked in, looking official and important.

"You go help them, Liz. I need to get going anyway. If I'm not there Wednesday, please tell the group how sorry I am, that I truly care about each and every one of them—it's just too hard for me right now."

"Okay," I said sadly. "But, Susan, you know these women. They'd want to share your burden. Why don't you let us try?"

Snatching her purse, Susan glanced around the coffee shop, shrugged her shoulders, and left.

I went to help my customers—two who wanted nothing from me other than my coffee. They wanted it hot, strong, and fast. And that's what they got.

The skies were darkening, clouds threatening to dump a load of heavenly tears on Portland streets. *Too much sorrow lately. Way too much sorrow. . . .*

Chapter Six

Susan's Route to Respectability

Carly was the first to arrive on Wednesday. "Liz, are you still available to go with me to Seattle this Sunday?"

"I'm planning on it." I'd cleared it with Bill and even planned to prepare two of his favorite foods—tuna casserole and carrot cake—since he'd have to eat alone.

"Good. Because I got a substitute for my Sunday school class, and I told Joe."

"You told Joe?" I asked. "He knows you're going up to find out what happened to Eric?"

"Not exactly," she said. "I told him I wanted to make a quick trip up to see my folks for the day. Mom and Dad's anniversary is next week, and, well, I wanted to take them a present."

"Carly, you lied—to Joe! How could you lie to Joe?" This didn't set well with me, and I was surprised, frankly, at Carly.

"I didn't really lie. I just left something out." She stamped her foot. "Oh, all right, I lied! I know it was wrong, but I didn't want him to worry about something as inconsequential as this."

"Inconsequential? You really think this is inconsequential?" Looking at Carly, I had plenty of things I wanted to say to her. I could feel indignation creeping up my spine, the hairs on the back of my neck tingling. Advice, strong as French Roast, was about to spill out of my mouth. Lucky for both of us, Emma and Mariah walked in the door. Susan was right behind them. As she passed by, she squeezed my hand.

When we were all seated, cups in hand, iced raisin scones on the tables, Carly made a couple of announcements.

"First I want to ask for your prayers. Liz has agreed to go with me this Sunday up to Seattle. We're going to try to find out what became of Eric and to learn if he needs any help. We'll leave around 8:00 in the morning and hope to get back by 8:00 in the evening."

Emma raised her hand to speak. We all looked at her, and Annie laughed. "Emma, you don't have to raise your hand. We're not in school."

"I know, but I'm always blurting things out. This time I thought I'd be more polite. So, if you don't mind my asking, Carly, what have you found out already? Are you going up there cold? Do you have any idea where he is? Is he in a hospital? Is he back with his mother?"

Carly held up her arms to fend off the questions, a wry smile on her lips. "Emma, you're probably not the only one wondering about those things—and I'm glad. I'm glad you care, about me and about events and people in my past.

"No, I'm not going up there cold. I've done some research on the Internet and also by phone. There were several listings with Eric's last name. I took a chance and phoned a Carol Endsmire. She turned out to be his mother. She didn't want to talk with me, especially about Eric; but at least I found out where she lives and have her phone number. That will be our first stop on Sunday. I'll try to convince her that I want to help Eric, not cause her any problems. Then Liz and I will take it from there."

"Does she know we're coming?" I asked. Somehow this seemed like a B movie to me. I was beginning to see Carly in a new light—frankly, not a flattering one.

"No, I was afraid she'd make it a point not to be there."

"What if she's not home?" Emma asked.

"Well, then, I guess Liz and I will have to follow up on a couple of other leads I unearthed. In any case, what we will need from you is your promise to pray that we'll go to the right places, say the right things, act as representatives of goodwill and reconciliation, and leave the rest to God."

The group agreed to pray for us, especially on Sunday.

"The second announcement I need to make," Carly said, "is that we're halfway through our stories. I've told you mine, Annie has shared hers, and so has Emma. That leaves Susan, Mariah, and Liz. Who would like to go next?"

• • • • •

"I'll go," Susan said, glancing at me, eyes brimming with tears. "I need to get this over with," she sniffed. "Bottom line is I need your help. I need your prayers, too." She sniffed again. "Liz knows—I almost quit the group just so I wouldn't have to talk about these things." Tears spilling from her eyes, Susan lay her head in her palms, elbows resting on her knees, and let out the pain she'd been stuffing for years.

On Susan's left, Mariah reached over and touched her arm. On her right, Annie put her arm around Susan's shoulder. The rest of us got up from our chairs and surrounded Susan, each one placing a hand on her. Normally, I'd have waited for Carly to take the lead, but not this time. From the depths of my heart, I prayed.

> Father God, Susan's in great pain. Help her to feel your presence here in our circle, to feel comfort in knowing that you're here, that you'll never leave or abandon her, that you'll give her grace and power to handle any problem she faces, that you have put her here in our midst so that we can help her as well. Amen.

We waited silently as Susan took some deep breaths. Wiping her eyes, she took a sip of the water Carly had brought from the kitchen. While Susan worked to compose herself, our little group saw a different Susan from the one we'd come to know.

She had always appeared to be a woman of unusual grace and poise. Not especially demonstrative, she seemed distant at times, yet always kind and thoughtful. She rarely talked about her family or her past—seeming more comfortable listening to others and offering helpful insights. Susan was as put together as the rest of us hoped to be one day . . . and now this. What else was there about Susan that we didn't know?

• • • • •

"Till now, I've been selective about what I've told you. Not knowing you more than a few months, I didn't feel I could bare my soul to you. I don't bare my soul to anyone really, never have. One time I did and regretted it almost immediately when my confidence was betrayed and I became a laughing stock at school. So, till now I chose to only tell the parts of my story that would make me sound good, make me sound like a victim that you would want to love and protect."

"We all do that," Emma broke in, apparently trying to comfort Susan but, in the process, betraying herself. I wondered what Emma could possibly have left out of her story, or Annie, or Carly.

"Let her talk," I said.

"Yes," Susan said. "Let me talk while I have the courage."

• • • • •

I realize that most of what I've told you about myself revolves around my Uncle Bob. Bob is my mother's oldest sibling, and what he did to me took her totally by surprise. To her, he'd always been the model big brother, the only one in her family who'd ever paid much attention to her, helping her with her studies, tutoring her in math every Tuesday after football practice. She thought the world of him.

I guess we'll never know what prompted him to strike out at her by sexually abusing her daughter. That's the way she saw it anyway; and that's what made it so difficult for her when she discovered his treachery and my "complicity" in not telling her. Believe me, I wanted to tell her. I wanted someone to intervene for me. But, as I think I told you before, Uncle Bob had threatened to hurt us if I ever spoke a word to anyone. So I kept silent—out of fear.

But Mother could never see it that way, and from then on, there wasn't a thing I could do right. I couldn't be trusted . . . that's all there was to it. She wouldn't believe a thing I said, challenging my motives at every turn, shutting me out of her world. I was no longer worthy to approach her heart.

After a while, I began to identify with the low expectations she had of me, to feel that perhaps she was right, that I was duplicitous and couldn't be trusted. Having accepted that picture of myself, I began to live it out. The friends I chose, the activities I engaged in, the lies I told—all reflected my low self-esteem.

By the time I reached my teens, I had already been involved in petty theft, drunkenness, carousing, and fist fights. Mother felt vindicated, that she'd been right about me all along, that I was truly a bad seed.

As I got older, I chased around, dropped out of school, slept with many men, got pregnant, and had the abortion I told you about. And here, my friends, I have to ask your forgiveness. I lied about the abortion. That, for once, was not Uncle Bob's fault. I just made that up, combining two miserable points in my life. Please forgive me.

• • • • •

Susan looked slowly around the group and saw by our nodding heads that we did, indeed, forgive her. *Who are we to cast stones when we, too, have covered up things in order to protect ourselves? Who could doubt that Susan had her reasons when she lied to us? She hardly knew us then—now she was coming clean.*

• • • • •

I've been so ashamed of my past at times that I've done all I could to distance myself from it. I rarely think of my childhood or of my mother. She committed suicide ten years ago, leaving a note in which she said goodbye to every surviving relative, everyone except me and Uncle Bob. Uncle Bob. He's been associated with everything bad in my life, so I just paired him with my abortion, for simplicity's sake.

But the truth is, I got pregnant and I got the abortion. The abortion was a bad experience, but I was glad not to be pregnant anymore. I don't know who was more relieved, me or the men I was sleeping with. Not a single one of them had wanted to be the father of my child. Not a single man stepped up to protect me or my baby. Suddenly I didn't like men much anymore.

I decided to clean up my act. Quitting all my vices cold turkey, I set my sights upon a respectable life, a life where I could hold my head up high and stand tall. After completing the requirements for a G.E.D., I got an Associate degree in

Accounting at Clackamas Community College and found a bookkeeping job at an upholstery shop in Oregon City. I did my best to live an upstanding life.

One day while everybody else was on their lunch break, I was alone in the shop when a man came in with a dining room chair. "My mother has a set of six of these," he said, holding the chair firmly by the back. "She'd like to know the cost of re-upholstering the seats."

I explained that our estimator was on her lunch break and asked if he'd like to leave the chair. Betty would call him or his mother with a price. He agreed to leave the chair, along with his name and phone number.

When Betty returned from lunch, I gave her the information.

"I know this family," she said. "They live not far from me on South End Road. In fact, one of their sons has been in and out of trouble for years. What did this man look like?"

I described him to Betty—tall, slim, dark hair and eyes, probably thirty-five or thirty-six, good looking.

"That sounds like him; the age is right. He's a real flirt, did he come on to you?"

"No. Actually, he was very nice, a gentleman. He didn't seem interested in me at all."

"Was he wearing a ring?"

"Frankly, I didn't pay any attention."

"Just as well. If this guy is who I think he is, he is certainly not your type."

"What do you mean by that, Betty?" I asked. "What type am I?"

"You know . . . respectable. I can't see a girl like you being interested in someone like Ed Reynolds."

I was stunned. *Imagine that. Betty called me respectable. I wonder if that is how others see me.*

From then on life looked different to me. I began to stand straighter, take greater care in how I dressed and wore my makeup. *Perhaps I can do more with my life than working in this little upholstery shop. Maybe I should think about getting a job in Portland. There'd be more opportunities for advancement and also for meeting new people, people who were going places.*

Not one to waste time, I immediately began looking for employment in downtown Portland. While standing in line at the State Employment Division, I met a guy named Peter. He was nice enough. When his name was called, he left with a smile, leaving me to fill out my application.

I completed the necessary paperwork and secured an appointment for an interview later in the day. On leaving the Employment Division, I noticed Peter standing at a bus stop.

"How'd it go?" he asked. "Did you get a job?"

"Not yet," I answered. "How about you?"

"Nope. But at least I can say I tried. Hey, you want to go for coffee somewhere? I'm free for the rest of the day."

I had time to spare since my interview wasn't for two hours. "Sure," I said. "Where do you want to go?"

"Well, it will have to be within walking distance. Or we could hop on the Max and ride over the river to Lloyd Center. They have a good food court there."

"I'd better stay on this side of town. I have a job interview at 3:00."

Peter looked at me with a puzzled expression. "Wow, an interview! What are you trying to do—get a job?"

"That's the idea, isn't it?"

"That may be your idea." Peter said. Looking heavenward, he laughed. "I just need to act like I'm trying so they'll let me stay on unemployment."

I don't have time for people like this, I said to myself. *Peter would have fit into my past life but there's no room for him in my present one and especially not my future.* I turned to leave.

"Hey, what about coffee?" Peter asked, frowning.

"Changed my mind. Thanks anyway."

I found a fast food restaurant, ordered a salad, and spent the next hour and a half looking over my resume, trying to anticipate questions that might be asked in the interview.

Riding up the elevator in the Standard Plaza Building, I smiled to myself. *What will Mother think of me now? She always said I'd never amount to anything. Yet this bad seed finished school, went to college, and is about to apply for a bookkeeping job in a high rise in downtown Portland.*

The elevator door opened on the third floor and a gorgeous man stepped in. Dressed in a dark suit, white shirt, and deep red tie, he was the picture of success. Alone in the elevator, we glanced at each other and smiled, a little awkwardly. I felt butterflies but they were delicious. Suddenly, the elevator stopped again and two more people got on.

"Hi, Greg," one of them said, nodding to the hottie.

Greg. His name is Greg. Greg must work in this building because people know him. I wonder what floor he works on.

Greg got off on the eighth floor; I had to go to nine. *Well, if I get this job, at least we can ride eight floors together.* I chided myself. *Get a grip. You have an interview in ten minutes.*

The interview went well. I got the job—and my very own office overlooking Portland to the east. Mt. Hood rose in the distance, covered in a white blanket of new-fallen snow. *To think I will get to look at Mt. Hood each and every day! And, even better, I'll get to ride up and down the elevator with Greg.*

I gave the upholstery shop two weeks' notice. Those two weeks felt like two years, two years away from my Mt. Hood office and elevator rides with Greg. Looking back, I can hardly believe what a fool I was, acting like a school girl with her first big crush.

Yet, knowing I'd soon be moving on, I took to glancing around the upholstery shop, seeing many things for the first time: the homey clutter of fabric samples in a variety of colors and textures; upholstery tools neatly stacked in portable caddies, various chairs in process of getting fitted for a new cloth coat. In the showroom window, finished products—chairs and settees—waited to be transported home in all their glory.

I thought to myself, *I have been a humble chair waiting for my new cloth coat in Oregon City. Those days are nearly a thing of the past. Soon I'll be wearing furs in Portland.*

Had I known then what I know now, I'd have been grateful for the warmth of that new cloth coat. I'd have stayed in the cozy upholstery shop in Oregon City among people like Betty who knew me and found me "respectable."

But the allure of the high rise was too great. I was on my way up. *I am destined for great things, no matter what my mother thinks.*

• • • • •

Emma could contain herself no longer. "So how long was it before you ran into Greg again?"

"I was wondering about the fur coat." Annie gave the rest of us a wink.

"My fur coat wasn't the only dream that didn't materialize—but I'll get to that in a bit. To answer your question, Emma, we've got to go back to the Standard Plaza Building."

• • • • •

My first day, I saw Greg on the elevator. On the second day, I saw him in the employee lounge. On the third day, back in the elevator. On the fourth day, the elevator again. By Friday, he joined me in the employee lounge and walked me across the sky bridge to my bus stop.

The chemistry between us was unbelievable. We were finishing each others' sentences by the end of the month. People began to consider us a couple; I'd never been so happy.

Greg Garrett was a star on the rise, definitely on his way up the corporate ladder. He was merely a junior auditor but one that his CPA firm was grooming for middle management. They sent him to audit the books of their most important accounts, whether locally, regionally, or nationally. Like many up-and-coming executives, Greg had learned to say the right things, join the right clubs, and even attend the right church. All of his activities were measured by how advantageous they'd be to his career.

In one sense I was a liability, having only an Associate degree from a community college. But I was attractive and knew how to dress; so with some coaching in political correctness, I became Greg's own Eliza Doolittle. Soon I didn't need any help from my personal Professor Higgins—I became a real fair lady.

Greg was attracted to me physically, but because of my negative past experiences with men, I held him off. No wedding ring, no sex. When he could stand it no longer, he proposed one Saturday night, took me before a justice of the peace the following Friday, and to bed one hour later.

I'm sure my lovemaking was a disappointment to him. Sex had brought me only pain and sorrow, having been imposed on me as a child or performed outside the safety of marriage. It would take time to overcome my hang-ups.

Whether or not I enjoyed sex, the truth is that Greg and I were fertile myrtles: I conceived within four months of our wedding day. I was pleased to be pregnant, but he wasn't sure children fit into his career plans. In fact, he was downright certain a child would cramp our style financially.

"Would you consider abortion this time, Susan?" he asked. "We can get pregnant later."

Remembering the men of my past, I was crushed. *No one wants to have a child with me, not even my own husband.* I wanted to say, "No, I definitely would not consider abortion this time." But instead I said, "Whatever you think, Greg." I didn't tell him I'd already had one abortion. *What difference will another one make?*

Turns out it made a huge difference. This time when I'd read the pregnancy test as a married woman, I immediately began to entertain thoughts of what it would be like to be a mother. I'd already decided that I would be a good mother, loving and caring. No child of mine would ever hear the words I'd heard from my own mother, never feel the rejection she'd imposed on me. Yet Greg had asked me to perform the ultimate rejection—to deny my child the right to live. And, worse, I'd agreed to it.

I aborted our baby—went to the clinic, by myself, and came home alone.

Loathing filled my whole being, loathing for Greg and for myself. Poison spewed from my heart and into my words. The things I said to him were so hateful that I'm sure he was glad every time he was sent out of town on an audit. He probably asked for those assignments.

I can't tell you how many times we discussed divorce, so I was shocked one day when, out of the blue, Greg said he wanted us to try to have another baby. He said he was sorry that he'd suggested abortion. He asked me to forgive him. The fact that he was willing to put his career aside to save our marriage gave me hope. I agreed to try.

Shortly after I'd conceived, Greg revealed the real reason he'd wanted a child. The firm had promoted someone over him, and that person had a family. Sensing he'd move up the corporate ladder faster if he were a family man, Greg had impregnated me. Again, it was all about his career. I wanted to kill him.

Melissa was a healthy newborn, seven pounds, eight ounces, and twenty inches long. Beautiful, beautiful baby. But she was a girl. Greg felt that what he really needed was a son so he could brag about taking him fishing and coaching Little League. I told him he could do those things with Melissa, but somehow that wasn't the same. He wanted a son.

Sixteen months later Corey was born. Now Greg had something to crow about at the office. A promotion followed shortly thereafter and Greg was convinced that the two events were inextricably linked. Corey was Greg's little man.

We became two couples within a marriage: Melissa and Mom, Corey and Dad. It wasn't a good arrangement to be sure, but it kept everyone engaged. By the time Melissa was seven and Corey was five and a half, our little family was split right down the middle.

Favoritism is an ugly thing no matter how you slice it. Children know what's going on, and our children quickly learned how to manipulate their parents. For example, Melissa would decide she wanted a new bicycle so she'd tell Corey. Not wanting Melissa to get ahead of him, Corey would lobby for a bicycle from his dad. Greg, a softie where Corey was concerned, would always relent. Then Melissa would have grounds for a bicycle. After all, if Corey could have one, why couldn't she?

Their schemes worked because Greg and I were too busy with our own lives to discuss family matters. His total focus was on his career, and mine was split between my bookkeeping job and the children.

It didn't surprise me when Greg finally filed for divorce. The family man image was no longer quite so important now that he had achieved managerial status. In fact, he said he could go farther alone than he could with us holding him back.

"Holding you back!" I shouted at him. "When has anything or anyone ever held you back? You think of nothing but yourself and your career."

He looked at me blankly. "My only defense is that it's easier for me to be anywhere than here in my own home. I can't take any more of your anger and bitterness and sarcasm. You can blame everything on my ambition if you want. But you're one mean woman, Susan, and I'm just not interested in playing your games anymore." With that he stormed out of the house, and his only contact with us was through divorce lawyers.

I know there was truth in Greg's accusations. I had grown bitter and sarcastic after the abortion. I had neglected him, pouring myself into the children, particularly Melissa. But Greg had abandoned us all for his work—even Corey.

So where did that leave me? Suddenly, I became a single mother with two confused children who were angry with their father and even angrier with me because Daddy wasn't there and I was. Everything was my fault.

The children began to act out against each other. Corey hated Melissa because his daddy was gone but she still had me. It became all too clear that our children had come to view each other as pawns to get what they wanted from their parents. They had no love or respect for each other. They still don't.

Adding to the stress, we went from enjoying a comfortable lifestyle to barely getting by on my bookkeeper's salary plus what we get monthly from Greg. And since child support was based on his income ten years ago, our situation has worsened as the cost of living has risen.

It hurts all the more to see Greg living the "good life." Having climbed many more steps on his corporate ladder, he's up there so far he can't see us any more. He's got a new life, new wife, new family. Other than the checks that come from his account manager, we have no contact with him. Corey is very bitter. I guess we all are.

• • • • •

Annie cut in, "Susan, are you getting family counseling?"

"We tried that. Frankly, I didn't much care for the counselor we had. He wasn't good with the children. They hated going and, besides, my insurance didn't cover the sessions. I just let it drop."

"That's not right!" Emma cried. "Insurance companies should cover something so important. There's no way families with financial problems can afford to pay high hourly fees."

"There were some free clinics available," Susan said, "but they didn't meet at times that worked for us."

"If the kids are as troubled as you say, it may be a good thing to seriously consider," Annie said. "But, please, I didn't mean to interrupt you. Go on with your story."

• • • • •

My work hours are such that the children get home from school before I do. Against my better judgment, I dispensed with day care a few years back when Melissa was thirteen and Corey was eleven. I know many would think they were too young to be left alone—and I agree now. But funds were tight and I had good neighbors, so I convinced myself that they'd be all right. That was my mistake.

I gave the kids a detailed list of instructions on what to do and what not to do after school, and I told them to call me at work for any reason. At first all seemed well. Then I began to relax, to get comfortable with our situation. That was another mistake.

Parent-Teacher conferences became painful experiences as disciplinary problems became a regular topic of discussion. The children's marks, though never remarkable, were sliding toward average and below.

Of course, I talked with the kids. Encouraged them to try harder. Reminded them that we were a team and we needed to work together as a team, each of us doing our part. Assured them that I'd rather be home with them, but since I couldn't, we all had to buck up and try harder.

At that, Melissa rolled her eyes and let out a deep sigh. Corey turned his back on me and left the room. "Corey, come back here!" But he didn't, and I realized then and there that I'd lost control. Melissa just looked at me and shook her head.

From that day on, life in the Garrett home has been no joy ride, and that's putting it mildly. Melissa began to invite friends in after school . . . lots of them, male and female. Our neighbor to the north let me know about the loud music that shattered the peace of the neighborhood. Well, I dealt with that. No more after school parties.

Then, despite my clear directions to the contrary, Melissa took to inviting one or two friends over, mainly girls. However, over time, that number was reduced to one—a boy, Tim.

Corey thought Tim was cool because he'd give him a dollar for ice cream at the grocery store. That left Tim and Melissa alone in the house. Need I say more?

If it hadn't been for a power outage shutting down operations at work, there's no telling how long these secret meetings would have continued. Walking in the house, I called out, "Kids, I'm home." No response, though I thought I heard some muffled noises coming from Melissa's room. "Melissa, Corey, where are you?"

"I'll be right out, Mom," Melissa called, breathlessly. "I'm just changing my clothes."

"Okay, honey," I said. "You left your sweater in the car this morning. Did you need it?" Not waiting for an answer, I opened the door to toss it on her bed, only to see a young man half-dressed, looking wildly around the room for his shirt.

Melissa's face turned from white to pink to red and she whispered sharply, "Tim. Go!" Tim grabbed the rest of his clothing and ran for the front door. I don't know if he finished dressing in the living room or just ran out of the house half naked. If the neighbor to the north was watching, she got an eyeful.

Looking defiant, Melissa challenged me. "Well, what did you expect? It's not my fault that you and Dad got a divorce. It's not my fault that there's no one here to take care of me and Corey."

"Where *is* Corey?" I asked, looking around for a place to sit, my head swimming. Only then did I notice that Melissa's room reflected her defiance, posters of angry rock stars glaring down at me, shelves with books turned every which way, on their sides, upside down. In the corner were stacks of dirty clothes. *Why have I not noticed this before?*

"Where's Corey?" I repeated.

"He went out."

"Out where? And why? You know he's not supposed to go out by himself."

Just then the front door opened and Corey came in, the remainder of an ice cream bar in his hand, the breath of cold air clinging to his clothes.

"Melissa, how could you have let your brother go out in the cold? And you, Corey! Where have you been?" I demanded.

"I just went to the store. I wasn't even gone half an hour."

"That's not the point. You're not supposed to leave unless I know about it. It's not safe for you to go out by yourself. And besides, it's freezing out there!"

"Whatever." Corey looked me straight in the eyes, shook his head, and turned on his heels, leaving the room.

"You come back here, young man!" I screamed, bounding after him. If he'd been younger, I'd have paddled him; but now I found myself looking eye to eye with an angry preteen who had no qualms about defying me.

"What do you want from me," Corey shouted, "an apology? Well you're not going to get one." His dark eyes filled with hatred and he continued, "Thanks to you, I have no Dad, no money, nothing. Yet you expect me to 'buck up and try harder.' Why don't you buck up and try harder? Find a better job. Make more money. Leave me and Melissa alone."

Melissa came and stood beside Corey. It was a face-off—them against me—an unlikely alliance against a common enemy, their mother.

• • • • •

"That was four years ago," Susan said with a sigh. "Annie, you're exactly right. I should have pursued family counseling. But I didn't. And things went from bad to worse."

"It may not be too late," Annie said. "I can look in the referral box at work. There are family counselors listed in there. Let me help."

"What about some personal counseling, Susan?" Carly asked. You've been carrying a heavy load all these years, and it doesn't sound like you've been receiving any positive feedback. How are you holding up? We had no idea all this was going on in your life. You always seem so strong."

Susan looked around the room at each of us. Dropping her head, she whispered, "Strong? I'm not strong. It's all an act." Shaking her head, she slumped down in her chair, the picture of defeat. "I haven't allowed anyone inside my real world. It's too painful even for me; why would I want to force it on anyone else?"

Susan looked deeply sorrowful as she glanced at us one by one. "I can't believe I'm telling you all of this." Then she added, "But in a strange way, it feels good."

Crossing her legs and taking a deep breath, Susan continued her story.

• • • • •

Those were difficult times. I tried the best way I knew to love my kids, but they shut me out of their lives. Melissa and Tim soon broke up, and she dated a number of other guys, types my mother would have called "creeps" and I'd have to agree with her.

One fellow she dated was an abuser. I sensed that about Jordan immediately and tried to warn Melissa. There was something about the way he dominated her, trying to control her activities, her friendships, even her thoughts. Like many girls, Melissa mistook these attentions as a sign that Jordan deeply loved her, so much so that he wanted to know everything about her, what she did, where she went, who she went with.

Fortunately, Melissa recognized the truth about Jordan before things had progressed beyond threats and a few bruises. Although it was a difficult lesson for Melissa to learn, it did have a positive effect—it brought us together again.

She came to me, arms outstretched, tears in her eyes. "Mother," she choked. "Can you ever forgive me?" As she started to list her many transgressions, I took my baby in my arms, saying, "Hush, my darling." We clung to each other until the tears stopped.

To this day, I can still breathe in the sweet air of repentance and forgiveness. I can open my eyes and see blue skies where only hopeless gray ones had covered my world. I can still feel my daughter's heart beating close to mine and sense that there's hope beyond the present, hope for a future of understanding and togetherness.

These are the things that keep me going because, as difficult as Melissa had been, and continues to be at times, Corey has been far worse. And he's not yet sixteen. Sometimes I fear he's headed for the penitentiary. The only person he really wants is Greg, and Greg has continued to show no interest in his son. Poor Corey doesn't know how to deal with the rejection, so he strikes out at anyone and everyone.

Just this past week Mrs. Baker, the principal from Corey's school, called and asked me to come at once, if possible. I dropped everything and was there in forty-five minutes. Along with some other boys, Corey had been accused of harassing freshmen in the boys' bathroom. Of course, he denied it. When Mrs. Baker pressed a little too hard, Corey came out slugging. I think he would have hit her except for the fact that the wrestling coach was in the office and intervened. He took Corey down the hall to give me and the principal time to talk.

As I glanced around her office, I saw photographs of former students who currently attend colleges and universities around the nation. Smiling, intelligent, forward-looking—young people with a future. *What makes some turn out like that while others become rebellious, antagonistic, angry, young people with no apparent goals?*

Mrs. Baker saw me looking at those pictures. "Fine young students," she said. "Our country's future leaders."

I glanced down, not wanting to meet her eyes. A tear spilled, dropping to my feet.

Smiling, Mrs. Baker came to me and said kindly, "May I?" as she placed her arm around my shoulder. "Corey is very smart. His picture should be on my wall in three or four years. But he's angry. He needs a father figure."

"I know," I said, "but there's no one."

Mrs. Baker quietly cleared her throat. "Mr. Edwards, the wrestling coach you just met, is willing to spend time with Corey, to work with you in providing what Corey needs."

"Why would he do that? Why would he care?" In the back of my mind I felt suspicious of any older man wanting to befriend my boy.

"There are many good men and women in the teaching profession, Mrs. Garrett, people like Jerry Edwards who want to see their students succeed. Mr. Edwards lost his son in a tragic accident several years ago. Since that time, he has looked out for boys who need a dad."

I hung my head, ashamed of my suspicions. "I would be so grateful," I said. "I've not known what to do with Corey."

"It's settled then. I'll tell Jerry—Mr. Edwards—to call you and arrange a meeting."

She walked me to the door, extending her hand. My eyes swimming in tears, I took her hand and grasped it hard. "You're a lifesaver. I can never thank you enough. God bless you."

On my way home from that meeting at the school, I swung by the coffee shop and talked with Liz. I was going to quit our group because I couldn't imagine things getting any better and, frankly, I didn't want to rehash the particulars of my life. I just wanted to crawl into bed and pull the covers over my head.

But, actually, that day became a turning point for us. Later that afternoon, Mr. Edwards called and then came over. He brought references from Mrs. Baker, two teachers, and his pastor.

"I want you to be comfortable with my spending time with your son," he said. "Working at the school, I've had background checks, and want to assure you that I'm no pedophile."

Thank You, God, for calming my heart. We hammered out the details of his meetings with Corey and discussed how the two of us could be involved in helping my son.

I'm feeling encouraged and, even better, Corey seems more relaxed and somewhat hopeful. A macho man old enough to be his father, a wrestling coach no less, has shown some interest in him. This is a very positive step, one that started me thinking about all the missteps I've taken.

I've thought about my life and how it measures up against those hopes and dreams I had when I was younger. All I ever *really* wanted was to get beyond my miserable childhood, the sex abuse, the carousing, and the abortion. I wanted to be "respectable."

I can see now that, though Greg used me to get what he wanted, in retrospect, I did exactly the same thing. He was my "ticket to respectability." At the time, I thought respectability meant living in a big house, driving expensive cars, wearing fancy clothes, joining the best clubs, and meeting the right people. I thought it meant finally winning my mother's approval.

Did I get these things? No. Instead I got my kids—and a new point of view.

I'm learning that riches aren't essential to a respectable life. Respectability, at least to me, means that you're true to yourself and to those you love. It means you don't give up on life but press on despite the difficulties.

When I wake up in the morning, my first thoughts are of my children. I wonder what we will experience on this day. Will there be anger? Or will there be a hint of a smile on Corey's face when I place steaming pancakes in front of him, slathered with syrup? Maybe Melissa will reach out and gently poke her brother when he does something goofy, like snort or fall off a chair. And if not on this day—then maybe someday soon.

I will not give up on my kids. Their childhood has been hard—in some ways as hard as mine was. But they will never hear their mother say they aren't any good or that they won't amount to anything. Because I know that simply isn't true. Time is on our side, and now we have a principal and a wrestling coach to help us.

So, no, Annie. I never got the fur coat. And I'll be perfectly content with my cloth coat, as long as Melissa and Corey turn out all right. And if they ever ask me what I think about climbing corporate ladders or taking elevators to offices with views of Mt. Hood, I'll tell them all of that is fine—as long as they keep their feet on the ground.

• • • • •

Susan smiled, took a deep breath, and reached over for her coffee which, by now, was stone cold. I quickly took her cup to the kitchen and dumped out the old before pouring a steaming refill. When I returned, the girls were all clustered around Susan.

"Oh, Susan," Emma cried. "You're my hero! Can I come and live with you?"

"I thought *I* was your hero, Emma!" Annie bellowed.

We all laughed.

"You are. You both are. I'll live with you half the time and Susan half the time. And the rest of the time I'm coming to live with Liz."

"Well, if you come to live with me, we're going to have to work on your math," I said laughing. Turning to Susan, I added, "Thanks for trusting us enough to open up your life to us. That had to be difficult for you after keeping it inside for so many years."

"It wasn't as bad as I'd thought it would be," Susan said. "In fact, you all made it almost easy. Now that you know, would it be okay if I call you now and then for prayer?"

"Of course."

It was getting late—time to call it a night. "With that, I'm going to shoo you all out of here," I said. "I've got cleaning people coming in the morning and I've got to get things ready for them. You don't think I keep this place looking spankin' clean all by myself, do you?"

Left alone in the shop, I drew the shades, dimmed the lights, and played soft music, thinking all the while how blessed I was to be part of this group of women. Like the tables and chairs I was stacking in the corner, some of us had been backed into corners ourselves. Either through our own poor choices or through the poor choices of others, we'd been pushed around, knocked down, and bruised. But, by the grace of God, we'd been raised up and given the courage to try again.

It's good to be alive, I thought, and I began to whistle while I worked.

CHAPTER SEVEN

A TRIP TO SEATTLE

In the morning the cleaning crew came. While they were hard at work, I was glad for a few precious hours to think . . . about Susan's story, about my upcoming trip on Sunday with Carly, about my life with Bill and our relationship with our daughters.

I needed to evaluate some of my choices. *Are they in keeping with all I hold dear? Am I, like Susan, being true to myself and to those I love? Am I leading a "respectable" life?* Most of all, I needed to try, once again, to discover the blessed freedom that others in the group have found. Why does it elude me? Maybe today, in the privacy of my own thoughts, I could find some answers.

I've got this cubbyhole behind the kitchen, just large enough for a padded folding chair and TV tray. There's one small shelf at waist level with room for my gooseneck lamp, a wind-up clock, my Bible, and a notebook. There's another small shelf on my left with space enough for a carafe and cup of coffee. I can enter my cubby, pull a sheet of plywood across the entrance, sit down in my chair, and escape the world. And that's just what I planned to do.

A candy bar in one pocket, a bottle of water in another, pen and paper in hand, I squeezed into my tiny alcove and pulled the plywood door shut behind me. Reaching for the carafe, I filled the cup I'd left there previously and settled down on my folding chair. *Blessed quietness. An entire day of blessed quietness. Where would I begin?*

Susan came immediately to mind. Like all of us, she'd had her share of trials and tribulations. I've been told that raising children alone is one of the hardest things in life, and I have no reason to doubt that. Raising children as a couple can be hard, so trying to do it alone? I can only guess.

I was glad for the principal and wrestling coach at Corey's school, but I also felt the Garrett family could benefit from family counseling. I decided to talk to Bill. Since finances were a problem, maybe we could help. Bill would have been a great role model for Corey, but it looked like Mr. Edwards was filling that need.

Carly's friend Eric came to mind. I wondered how things would have been different if he'd had a positive male role model or, even better, if his dad hadn't deserted the family. I wondered if we'd find him when we went to Seattle, or if we'd at least uncover some news that would give Carly closure.

Carly should have told Joe the real reason she was going to Seattle. I decided to tell her so. Keeping something like this from him could come back to bite her if he ever found out. I believe in being honest about things. Anyway, why would Joe feel threatened by Eric? Eric was totally out of the picture by the time Carly met Joe. Carly's usually so honest and straightforward. I wondered what was motivating her to be so devious about this and hoped I'd be able to help her sort out her feelings.

I opened my Bible and read from the book of James. "If any of you lacks wisdom, he should ask God, who gives generously to all without finding fault, and it will be given to him." Laying my head on the makeshift desk, I prayed for wisdom in dealing with Carly. And, as often happens when my head is down and my eyes are closed, I fell asleep.

I must have slept for over an hour. When I awoke, the shop was deathly quiet, the only sound being the ticking clock on the shelf. The cleaning crew had taken a break and the shop was empty of all but me and my thoughts. But I didn't want to think anymore. I wanted to get out and go shopping.

The Lloyd Center mall is just three blocks away. I could walk there, spend a couple of hours Christmas shopping, enjoy the crowds, and pick up Bill's favorite—caramel corn at the candy shop above the old ice rink. For years he and I would purchase a bag of it and munch away while we watched the ice skaters glide by below us. *It used to be such fun to watch the skaters at Christmas.*

The brisk walk did me good. Shoppers were thronging the mall and everyone seemed in fine spirits. Entering Macy's, I ran into Annie, who was taking a quick break from work.

"I'm looking for a trinket to give the girls in the H.E.A.R.T. group," she said. "I've been particularly worried about Mariah lately. She looks so sad. I was thinking about purchasing some friendship rings or charms or something. Have you got time to help me look?"

"Sure," I said, taking her arm. "They have a collection of Italian charms over on that counter. I was looking at them the other day. Either those or friendship rings are a really sweet idea, Annie."

"Don't you just want to mother Mariah, Liz? She and Emma are both such wonderful young women. As different as night and day."

"I know what you mean. I only wish Emma could give Mariah a dose of her self-confidence." I wandered over to a nearby watch counter.

"Liz, look at these charms!"

Annie's squeal of delight brought me quickly to her side, and instantly I saw what had caught her eye. On the counter lay tiny charms showing one hand grasping someone's wrist in a sign of victory, like a referee and a boxer, for example.

"Liz, I'll give these as a reminder to support one another and uphold one another in prayer. What do you think?" Her eyes full of excitement and hope, she looked to me for confirmation of her plan.

"I think it's a great idea. When will you give them out?"

"Christmas is two weeks away. I'll give them out next Wednesday. Maybe they'll help with the emotional turmoil that sometimes comes with Christmas."

"You thinking about Mariah again?"

"Yes, but also Susan. There's no telling what challenges she may face with Corey home from school all Christmas break." Annie looked at the clock. "Wow, I'd better pay and get back to work. I said I'd only be gone half an hour."

"Well, I'll let you take care of business," I said. "I've got to get back to the shop before the cleaners leave. Gotta pay them."

"I imagine they'll wait for you." Annie smiled.

I'd spent longer at the mall than I'd planned and got back to Over Coffee just as the cleaning crew was packing up. The shop looked wonderful, not a smudge in the place—sparkling windows, fresh curtains, scrubbed woodwork, and gleaming chrome fixtures. Someone had placed a potted poinsettia on the table by the door, along with an invoice.

"Looks like I made it back just in time to pay you," I said, looking around the shop. "Thanks for your good work. Everything looks terrific. When did you start leaving plants? That's a nice touch."

"It's a present from your husband. He stopped by about an hour ago."

"About the time I was buying him the caramel corn. We must have been on the same wavelength," I laughed. *Happens more and more the older we get.*

I paid the crew, and within five minutes they were gone.

Outside, the streetlights were coming on and it was only 4:00. *I'm out of here. Gotta go home and see my man, take him some caramel corn. That's the beauty of being your own boss. Good-night shop . . . see you in the morning.*

• • • • •

At 8:00 A.M. on Sunday, Carly knocked at my door. "Thanks for coming with me, Liz. I'd probably have backed out if not for you."

"That plus the fact that Emma will surely grill you on Wednesday about what we learn in Seattle."

"If she can wait that long!" We laughed as we piled into Carly's Toyota Camry and settled in for the three-hour drive to Seattle. "Excuse the backseat. I took the girls Christmas shopping last night and we stopped for fast food on the way home."

"Looks no different than our car did when the kids were young. Smells the same, too. Mmmmm yummy, French fries! I kind of miss that smell, the grease, the salt . . . all the good stuff that leads to high cholesterol and high blood pressure."

"You sound like my mom," Carly said.

"You mean old?" I laughed as I picked a French fry off the floor at my feet and tossed it in the back.

"I mean 'comfortable.' With you I feel comfortable."

Driving north, we chatted about the weather, the price of gasoline, world affairs, and Portland politics. We discussed the outlet stores along I-5 in Centralia and the growing numbers of casinos in the Pacific Northwest. As we approached Olympia's gleaming capitol dome on the hill, we became more focused on the purpose of our trip to Seattle.

"Liz, I didn't tell you and the group something—something about Eric and me."

"I figured there was more to the story," I said, keeping my eyes squarely on the road ahead.

"Other than Joe, he's the only man I ever slept with. But he was the first."

"Yes. And?"

"I know it's dumb, but I can't seem to get over the fact that I gave him something of myself that was very precious." She glanced over at me but said nothing more.

Silence. *Is she waiting for me to say something?*

"I mean I should have waited to give it to my husband."

"Yes, of course, Carly. But that's over and done with. You've been forgiven, set free, remember?"

"True. I have been forgiven, and I have been set free." She tapped her fingers on the steering wheel. "Nevertheless, I have to confess that I do, on occasion, still think about Eric."

"Oh?"

After an awkward silence, Carly said, "I fantasize about him, Liz."

"I get it. This is where you want me to let you have it, right? This is why you asked me to come, so I could tell you what a perfect idiot you are and insist that you turn this car around and go right back to Portland. Go right back to the safety of hearth and home. Am I right?"

"Well, should I?" She reached over and grabbed my arm.

"Why? So you can go back and fantasize some more?"

"What should I do, Liz?"

Remembering the verse from James, I sent up a quick prayer for wisdom and trusted that God would give me words of guidance. "What should you do? Well, it seems to me that, whether or not we go on to Seattle, you need to get some things settled in your mind before you return to your husband in Portland."

"Like what?"

"First, where are these thoughts of yours, these fantasies, coming from? Do you think they're good and honorable?"

"No."

"Then what?"

She held the steering wheel tightly, her face rigid. I heard her gulp. "They're vile and ugly and always leave me feeling guilty and horrible."

"Then where do you think they're coming from? Who is putting these thoughts in your head?"

"The devil, I suppose." Her voice trembled. "But once they start coming, I just can't seem to put them out of my mind."

"Well, that's a problem," I said. "These temptations to fantasize about another man are sinful thoughts that will put a wedge between you and Joe. You can't give in to them."

Carly began to cry. "I don't want to give in. I start thinking about Eric because I'm concerned about him. Yet it scares me that the concern can so easily run amok and have sexual connotations."

I'd heard enough. "Carly, I'm sure you've heard that these feelings are common, that when a young woman gives her virginity away, there's a strong bond that forms between her and her lover. Even when she moves on to someone else, or eventually marries, a part of her remains behind with that 'first one' and often leads to sexual fantasizing. Haven't you heard that?"

When she didn't answer, I said, "I could almost swear I heard you say that once to Emma."

"I did say it, Liz. And it's true."

"So . . . why are we going to Seattle? I mean, Carly, you have to look at your motives. Is this about Eric, or is this about you? If it's about you and your sexual fantasies, that's easy. Get over it. Repent, accept God's forgiveness, and move on. We go back to Portland.

"But if you really are concerned about Eric and feel you left something undone in terms of helping a friend, then we drive on to Seattle and see what can be done. You just have to be clear what this excursion is all about."

Carly looked across the seat at me. "Annie was right about you being a straight shooter. Okay if we keep driving north while I think about what you've said?"

Carly drove in silence before pulling over at the nearest rest stop. Taking her keys, she motioned for me to follow her to a picnic table. Her breath was visible in the cold December air. "Liz, it's freezing out here, isn't it! I'm so sorry," she laughed sheepishly. "What a flake I am. I've dragged you halfway across the State of Washington for something we could have discussed at Over Coffee in ten minutes."

I couldn't tell by Carly's expression whether she was mad, confused, resolute, or relieved. "What are you saying, Carly?"

"It's just that everything seems so clear now. I'm dealing with two separate issues, my own lustful thoughts—which I can confess without ever setting eyes on Eric again—and my concern for Eric's wellbeing, which I can deal with openly and honestly from Portland, with Joe's help. We don't need to go to Seattle on some kind of spy mission. My foolishness turned a good thing—caring about the welfare of another human being—into something shameful and secretive."

"Really?" I looked at her face and tried to discern the truthfulness of her words. Were her eyes clear? Yes. Was she hiding anything? Don't think so. "Is that how you really feel?"

"How I really feel is embarrassed and ashamed. Here I am the so-called leader of our support group, and I need the most support of all." Carly hung her head.

"I don't think that's true, but it's a good reminder that we all need one another. What do you want to do? Go home?" My teeth chattered, and I wished for a heavier coat.

"Let's go home." Carly stood and started toward the car.

"What will you tell Emma and the others?"

"I'll tell them that some lessons have to be learned more than once." Then she put her arm through mine, and we walked the rest of the way to the car.

A spirit of peace and relief flooded the Camry. We joked and teased and sang psalms, hymns, and a bit of Elvis, stopping along the way for fast food and—throwing caution to the wind—a giant order of French fries. Soon we were back in Portland with our families.

• • • • •

I'm sure Carly had some explaining to do to Joe, and I'm confident she did it well. I also know that Bill was glad to see me home so early because he gave me an enormous bear hug and waltzed me around the living room floor. We collapsed on the couch in gales of laughter.

Chapter Eight

Mariah's Search for Acceptance

On Monday, just as I was placing the open sign on the door, Emma called the shop. "How was Seattle? I couldn't reach Carly so thought I'd ask you. Did you find Eric? Was he all right? How's Carly?"

"Emma, darling," I said with exaggerated sweetness, "That is something you are most definitely going to have to ask Carly herself. And it would probably be prudent to wait until Wednesday to hear the entire story along with everyone else, don't you think?"

"Well, all right. So long as you make everyone else wait, too." I could detect just a hint of impatience in Emma's voice. Laughing, I promised not to let a single soul weasel a single fact out of me. A disappointed Emma hung up the phone with a veiled threat to hold me to my promise.

Within ten minutes, Mariah walked in and coyly pulled up a barstool. "You made it back from Seattle safely, I see. How was the trip?"

"Oh, just fine," I said, whistling as I scrubbed the counter. "You want coffee, or did you only come to snoop?"

"Coffee, please," Mariah feigned innocence, and for the first time *ever* she seemed to relax and join in the fun. A smile began at the left side of her mouth and spread all the way across her face. Her eyes twinkled and there, smack in the middle of her right cheek, was a glorious dimple.

"Mariah, where have you been hiding that dimple? It's absolutely wonderful. And your eyes are the color of sparkling sapphires. Honey, you're beautiful when you smile."

Self-consciously, Mariah looked up at me from her lowered eyes and pushed her glasses up on her nose. "Do you think so?"

"You are what they call a diamond in the proverbial rough. You've been hiding a buried treasure under all your gloom and doom."

Mariah quickly lowered her eyes again. "Don't make fun of me, Liz. I can't help it if I'm sad."

Realizing I'd offended her, I reached across the counter and took her hand. "Please forgive me, Mariah. I didn't mean to make light of your situation; I know it's difficult for you each and every day. But, *really*, you have beautiful features that I've never even noticed before. We must do what we can to accentuate them."

"How do we do that?" Mariah sat forward on her stool expectantly.

"We'll just have our own little makeover. Who do we know that's good at makeup and hairstyling? And what about wardrobe?"

Suddenly, Mariah's frown reappeared. "But I can't afford anything like that. I can barely pay my bills as it is. Besides, I didn't come here for that today. I just wanted to know how your trip was."

Handing her a cup of her usual boring decaf with cream, I said, "Like I told Emma, I'm not free to divulge that information. Carly will tell you all about it on Wednesday."

She looked up from her cup and smiled. "I wish I could have a makeover."

My brain was kicking into high gear. "There needn't be any cost involved. It would be something fun our group could do together. We could each get a makeover. Susan's a classy dresser. Carly, too. She's especially good at accessorizing from her years at Frederick & Nelson. Emma does a great job styling her own hair so maybe she could help us with ours."

"And Annie could teach us how to laugh." Mariah's dimple had returned along with the twinkle in her eye. *An amazing transformation!*

"Wait till we tell the others our idea on Wednesday night. It'll be so much fun!"

"Actually, I'm dreading Wednesday night," said Mariah, her smile gone. "I'm going to tell my story—I've decided it's time. I don't want to go last, and only you and I are left. Do you mind being last?"

"Not at all," I fudged. Actually I didn't plan to tell my story at all—not if I could figure a way to get out of it.

• • • • •

Annie and Susan showed remarkable restraint, neither of them calling before the meeting on Wednesday night. By the time Carly arrived, however, the group was already assembled, coffee distributed, cookies in hand, sitting at tables like a bunch of vultures waiting for scraps from the road trip to Seattle.

"This is a first, everyone here before the leader. What's the occasion?" Carly laughed, knowing full well she had center stage.

"Very funny," said Emma. "I've been waiting all week because Lizzie over there wouldn't spill the beans and you were never home."

"Liz wouldn't tell me anything either, Emma," Mariah said, passing the plate of biscotti to her friend.

"There, you see, dear Emma. I was true to my word. I said nothing to anyone. I am totally trustworthy, as you see." I looked at Carly just in time to duck a rolled-up napkin ball pitched at me from Emma's direction.

Mariah, laughing, jumped up, grabbed the napkin ball, and tossed it into the wastebasket behind me. Slam dunk!

"Whoa!" Annie gasped. "Was that Mariah who just slam-dunked a ball into the trash? Is that little Mariah standing there with a great big grin on her face?"

We all sat back in our chairs and gawked in surprise. Mariah, embarrassed by the sudden attention, shuffled her feet, dropped her head, and sat back down.

"No. No. Mariah, don't you dare retreat into your shell," Emma pleaded. "If this is the real you, come back. We'll love you either way, but we want to know who you are."

I looked at Mariah and then at the others. "Mariah revealed her other side to me earlier this week when she produced a beautiful dimple in her right cheek followed by a glimpse of sparkling blue eyes the color of sapphires. I proposed an idea to her. Shall I tell them, Mariah?"

She nodded.

I asked the group. "What do you think of this? Why don't we do makeovers for one another? We can start with Mariah."

"That sounds like fun," Emma squealed.

"I know about fashion and makeup," Susan offered.

"That's what I told Mariah," I said, nodding in Mariah's direction. "And I thought Carly could teach us all about accessorizing and Emma could work with our hair."

"What about me?" said Annie. "What can I bring to the table?"

"Can you teach me how to laugh?" Mariah said, taking off her glasses and looking earnestly at Annie.

"That's easy," Annie said. "I just look in the mirror."

"Oh, Annie!" Everyone groaned. "What are you talking about?"

"No, really, Annie," Mariah said. "I need to learn to laugh if I'm ever going to get out of the pit I'm in. And I want you to teach me how to be loving and kind without being a pushover." Mariah's frown returned, her glow disappeared, and I guess we all knew we had our work cut out for us.

"It's settled then," Annie said. "Next week, we'll begin our makeovers, and Mariah will be our first model."

"I can't believe you'd do all this for me. I've never felt so special." Getting up, Mariah came over and put her arm around me, whispering, "Thank you, Liz."

I whispered back, "You're welcome, Mariah." And then I asked her. "Do you want to tell your story now?"

"Not quite yet. I really do want to hear how things went with you and Carly in Seattle last Sunday. And I'm sure everyone else does, too." She looked around the room.

"You sure you want to wait, Mariah?" Carly asked.

"Yes, I'm sure."

"Okay, then. But I'm afraid you're all going to be disappointed. In fact, none of you are going to find this very exciting," Carly said, with a glance in my direction.

Emma picked up another napkin, rolled it in a ball, and hurled it in Carly's direction. "Quit teasing us! Did you find Eric?"

Picking up the napkin, Carly unfurled it slowly, and said, "No, but I found someone else. I found myself—or, I should say, a more grown-up version of myself."

Then she confessed that her ongoing thoughts of Eric had been tied up with regret and lust and immature fantasies. "That was sinful," she said. "What I need to do is separate all of those feelings from the fact that it's okay to care about a wounded person in my past. Helping Eric could be a good thing; but I must do it for the right reasons and without false pretenses—and I must include Joe in my plans. As my husband, he's my protector and provider, and he can be trusted to know if, when, and how much to help."

"So, have you talked to Joe about this, Carly?" I asked.

She nodded and dipped the end of her biscotti in her coffee. "Yes, actually, I talked to him about it when I got home on Sunday afternoon. He couldn't believe we were home already and wanted to know what happened." With a look of embarrassment, Carly related, "You see, I had told Joe that Liz and I were going up to surprise my parents for their wedding anniversary."

"Carly, you lied?" Mariah asked with a frown.

"Yes, Mariah, I lied. And I'm not proud of it. I had to tell Joe I lied and why." With a shrug of her shoulders and a tilt of her head, Carly's voice cracked as she said, "He put his arms around me, rested his head on top of mine, and just . . . sighed. What else would I expect?"

Mariah whispered so softly that only those closest to her could hear. "Rick would have beaten me for that."

Everyone was silent. We all knew what it was like to be caught in our own schemes. Yet not all of us knew what it was like to be loved so unconditionally, not by a flesh-and-blood person anyway.

"Joe said he'd help me find out what happened to Eric, that we would go to Seattle within the month and make an end to this. If there's any way we can remedy any of my own wrongs where Eric is concerned, we'll do that. If there is any way we can help Eric anonymously, we'll do that. Joe isn't interested in any further involvement with Eric, but he knows it's important to bring closure to this whole episode in my life."

"Joe's a saint!" sighed Emma. "Why did God make so few perfect men like Joe?"

"I agree Joe's wonderful and I'm lucky to have him," Carly said. "But, like I've told you before, he would be the first to say that he is not perfect. He can be disarmingly slow in his decision-making, he sucks his teeth, keeps the neighborhood awake with his snoring, and he laughs too loud—at *everyone's* pathetic jokes, not just mine."

She shrugged her shoulders and smiled. "But I will tell you this about Joe, and it's the thing that I most honor about him—he's honest. He's honest through and through . . . deception has no place in his life. Positioning himself to win never occurs to him. Cruelty never occurs to him. He's a good man."

"What do you think makes him like that, Carly?" Annie said.

"I have an idea," she said, "although I can't say for sure." She rubbed the side of her face and rested her fingertips on her temple, as if thinking.

We waited.

"Joe trusts God," she said at last. "He simply commits his way to the Lord and waits for him to work things out. That eliminates any need for conniving or manipulating, and it enables Joe to keep on doing good things."

Susan shook her head and sighed, "If only I'd known such things when I was trying to claw my way to the top in Portland!"

"Me, too," Annie said. "My life would have been a lot different if I'd learned to trust God early on."

"We've all learned some hard lessons in our lives," Carly said, looking at each of us. "For me, the events of this past weekend have raised the bar. I know I need to grow up, stop living in the past, stop thinking about things that were wrong in the first place, set my mind on things above, on things that are honorable and worthy of praise. I know I need to set a good example for my children to follow, honor my husband, and honor God by my life.

"So that's the end of my story," Carly said, pointing to me, "except to say that I wouldn't be experiencing this growth spurt if it weren't for Liz. She saw through my twisted thinking and set me straight," Carly said with a smile. "I'll keep you posted on any future events."

Carly gave me a big hug and led the others in a group cheer for me. I looked around at my pals. *So nice to be appreciated by friends!* Then motioning to Mariah, I asked, "Mariah, are you ready now?"

With fear in her eyes, she said in a soft voice, "Yes, I'm ready." She looked at the circle of friends. "I didn't want to be last, so I told Liz tonight was my night. She'll go next."

"Not if I can help it," I joked. Five pairs of eyes turned as one to look at me, and they weren't smiling. In them I saw a mixture of surprise, confusion, and hurt. I later came to realize that my flip response had devalued the importance of sharing their stories. I'd never meant to hurt them, but I did.

I tried to undo the damage I had done. "No, I just mean that your stories are so good, so . . . so wonderful. And your stories relate to one another. And you all, I mean we all, have been blessed by your revelations and your freedom and the forgiveness you've found." I held out my arms to them, pleading, "Oh, don't pay any attention to me. It's Mariah's turn. I'm not till next week."

"You promise? You promise you'll share next week?" Emma spoke for all of them. "It's important, don't you see, for you to open up to us too."

"I promise," I said, trying to conceal my embarrassment. "Now can we all turn our attention to Mariah?"

• • • • •

Mariah stood and walked over to the window, peering through the curtains. *What's she looking at? Who's she looking for?* She circled the group before returning to her chair, sat down, bit her lip, nodded her head, and began to tell us the story of her life—the story of a little girl who was never allowed to grow up, a little girl who found herself at the age of thirty-two afraid to make a decision. Like victims of Chinese foot binding, Mariah was unable to stand solidly on her own two feet because she had been bound tightly by the strange beliefs of her mother.

• • • • •

My mother always wanted a son. She had no use for girls, said we were a drain on society, would never amount to anything, would never earn the big paychecks. She'd pinned her hopes on a male child who could help her achieve a higher status in life.

In a way, I feel sorry for her. She's very bright and, with an education, she could have realized a lot of her dreams. But where she grew up, not much emphasis was placed on higher education, not for girls anyway. Her parents saw to it that her brother went to college, but my mother was expected to marry after high school or else get a job.

She married the week after high school graduation. It was an unhappy marriage that lasted long enough to produce me before they "split the sheets"—that's what Mother calls it. She worked long hours in retail to put food on our table. Some of my earliest memories are of her coming home, angry, shouting, kicking over kitchen chairs. I learned to stay out of the way, cowering behind the couch.

As I got older, I observed that her rage was directed against male supervisors who, in her opinion, weren't worth the paper their checks were written on. She said she could run circles around any of them, and they knew it. She said that they were able to advance simply because they were men. One day she looked at me and said I was destined to poverty and that she wished I'd never been born.

Mariah stopped talking long enough to take a deep breath and a swallow of water. Then, blinking back tears, she pushed her glasses back up on her nose and continued.

Some mothers might have felt differently. They might have tried to run interference for their daughters, opening doors for them, encouraging them on to higher education. But these things didn't occupy my mother's mind. She, instead, became a champion of causes with hope for success.

Was there a need in the inner city? She'd attend Town Hall meetings and become a spokesperson for that need. Was there an unjust regulation on the city books? She would campaign against that regulation, getting her name in the papers and on television nightly news.

The wider her fame or notoriety—whatever you want to call it—spread, the angrier she got. For all her renown, we were still nearly penniless. Her efforts weren't rewarded monetarily as, she believed, they would have been for a man.

I certainly was no advantage to her then, nor would I ever be. She began to look at me as a millstone around her neck. First, she had to work to support me and then she had to leave her civic meetings early to put me to bed. I heard about it when she came home.

I was about ten years old when my mother decided it was time for me to get a job. She arranged to take in ironing for the neighbor up the street. I'm sure the neighbor thought mother would be pressing her clothes—I doubt she'd have trusted a kid with her ironing.

I didn't mind the work because I wanted to help. Besides, I liked the smell of the steam as it curled up from the iron and the smell of sprinkled dish towels and handkerchiefs when the hot iron touched them.

But Mom never showed me how to adjust the heat settings for a woman's silk blouse. Of course, you can guess what happened. I scorched it—badly. I took a beating for that one, the first of many beatings.

I think Mom shocked herself the first time she slapped me. But before long, the beatings became regular. In an odd sense, I became her "whipping boy." Whenever things went wrong, she'd beat me. Whenever things went right, she'd beat me because things were sure to turn sour tomorrow. Whenever I made a mistake, she'd beat me to show me the error of my ways. Whenever I did something right, she'd beat me lest I become prideful.

Once, a well-meaning teacher reported my bruises, and I was rewarded with more beatings, only now the bruises were well hidden under my clothing. I was threatened with death itself if I revealed them to anyone. I learned to keep silent, to avoid other peoples' eyes. I learned to disappear in a crowd, to become a faceless, voiceless phantom mingling among the living.

Mariah's face had turned ghostly white, her large horn-rimmed glasses dominating the top half of her face. Her lips quivered and her head seemed to hang to the side as if she'd just been struck a blow. She looked out from under her glasses, cleared her throat, and continued her story.

As I grew older, Mother stayed out later and later at her civic meetings, not needing to come home to put me to bed. When she did finally come home, she would often bring a woman friend with her, and they would talk into the night. The next morning, Lois would still be there and would go to work directly from our house. Eventually, she moved in with us.

Lois lived with us for two years. She was nice enough, but she often made me feel uncomfortable. Sometimes she was kind and sympathetic, treating me like I wished my mother would. But other times she had a way of getting too close to me, and I didn't like the way she watched me when I was dressing.

I was about fourteen years old when Lois left. I was never sure what caused the rift, but I do remember my mother going into one of her tirades, yelling, kicking chairs, throwing things. That was the last we saw of Lois.

Shortly after that, a boy named Danny moved in next door. He lived with his folks and was a year ahead of me. Sometimes we would walk the three blocks to school together, and sometimes not. It all depended if there were other boys in the area—Danny didn't want to be seen with a girl. If a boy would suddenly appear, Danny would speed up and instruct me to slow down so that we wouldn't seem to be together. He was funny that way.

One day, coming home from school, we took a shortcut through someone's yard and were attacked by an enormous black and white dog. He'd crouched behind us and snarled, his white fangs glistening with spit. Danny began to run and the dog chased him, grabbing his ankles with powerful jaws. I screamed for help, but no one came. I grabbed at the dog's collar, but he only tightened his grip on Danny's ankle. I didn't know what to do, so I ran into the alley looking for help, or at least something to hit the dog with.

Finding an axe handle propped against a garage, I ran back to Danny and began to hit the dog over the head. Then the dog turned, bared his fangs, and leapt toward me. He caught me by the hair and was reaching for my throat when I heard a loud POP. The dog fell to the ground at my side.

Standing in the alley just behind the garage was an old man in a tattered red hunting shirt, a cap perched on his head. "Looks like I come along in just the nick of time." He chuckled and cocked his rifle. "I been wantin' to shoot that durn dog for years. He won't threaten nobody no more."

Danny's leg was badly chewed up—it took 112 stitches to close the wounds. Then there was the infection. Once that passed, he had a limp. We wondered if he'd ever be the same. Eventually he was, only he was never the same toward me.

The shortcut home had been my idea. It was my fault we got attacked by the dog. Danny knew it, his friends knew it, and my mother knew it. Now instead of just her thinking I was a useless piece of trash, several people thought so. My name was mud.

I couldn't hold my head up at school. No one would speak to me. No one would give me a chance to explain myself or even to express how bad I felt about Danny. Solitude became my only companion, so, at age fifteen, I invented an imaginary friend, Polly.

Polly went wherever I went. She didn't say much, but then neither did I. We just understood each other, without words. Sometimes I'd pour my heart out to her, like some people do in a diary. It gave me some relief.

One day, walking home from school—with Polly, of course—I heard someone whisper from the bushes. "Psst. Mariah. Come over here. I have something to tell you."

"Who are you?"

"It's me, Danny, and I want give you something."

Danny was talking to me again. A wave of relief spread over my body. But why was he hiding in the bushes? Probably, he didn't want to be seen with a girl. So without hesitation, I ducked behind the shrubs. "Hey, Danny!"

Danny wasn't alone—some of his friends were waiting for me. They raped me, all the while saying this was payback for the dog. Danny said I should be grateful this was the payment they had chosen, and that after this our accounts would be even. I could go back to school and everyone would leave me alone . . . .

• • • • •

Mariah stopped in mid-sentence as if trying to remember. Then, shaking her head, she looked at me and wiped the corner of her eye with her finger. I snatched the box of Kleenex from the counter and handed her a tissue.

"Thanks, Liz," she said.

I wondered if she wanted to stop, or at least take a break, but before I could suggest anything, she straightened her sweater and continued.

• • • • •

Leave me alone? Not as simple as that. I got pregnant. And I didn't know what to do—so I did nothing. When I could no longer hide my protruding stomach, my mother demanded the truth. She called me a slut, drove me to the Lovejoy Clinic, and told them to "get it done."

I didn't object. You don't object to my mother. I cried for days.

I didn't know for sure what I was crying about, I just knew that something was terribly wrong with this whole picture—my life, my mother, Danny, the rape, the pregnancy, the abortion, the baby. My baby! Life hadn't been fair to us, not fair at all.

I decided to name the baby Polly, after my imaginary friend. Only my baby was not imaginary, she had been a part of me, and now she was gone. "Polly, Polly," I'd whisper in my bed at night, "Where have you gone? Where are you now?"

For the next few months, I pondered those questions.

• • • • •

We were all crying by then for we had come to understand why Mariah was the way she was—insecure, immature, afraid to stand out. Like a beautiful bisque doll that's been dropped too many times, Mariah was shattered in body and spirit.

Emma got up from her chair and went to Mariah, putting her arms gently around her. "Oh, Mariah," she cried. "Was there no one to protect you—no one to give you hope?"

Mariah seemed shocked at Emma's display of affection. "Oh, don't cry for me, Emma. I found a wonderful friend. I was just going to tell you about her."

Emma pulled her chair near Mariah's and listened as she continued her story.

• • • • •

Near my school was a large brick church. The side door was open one day, so I went in. Kneeling in a pew toward the front was an old nun, dressed all in black with a white collar. I don't know what possessed me, but I walked up to her and knelt down beside her.

"May I help you, child?" the nun asked kindly.

"No. I just wanted to be near you—if you don't mind."

"Of course, I don't mind. You just stay here as long as you like. Would you prefer to sit?" She sat down on the bench and patted the seat beside her.

I sat. There was peace in that building sitting beside that old woman, a peace that passed anything I'd known in my life. I felt safe there, as if all the bitterness and strife that plagued me were a thing of the past.

"What is your name, child?" she asked me.

"Mariah."

"Have you come seeking forgiveness from God, Mariah?"

"I don't know how to ask forgiveness," I said, looking at her mournfully, my heart about to burst for my many failures. "And how can God forgive me in the first place? He doesn't even know me. And I don't know him."

She patted my hand. "God knows everyone. He knows all about you, Mariah. Whatever is on your heart, he knows, but he'd like to hear from your own lips what your needs are."

With her silky-soft face and baby-blue eyes, this gentle woman won my trust at once. She seemed to know God, and she was saying that he knew me. Not only that, but he wanted me to talk to him, to tell him what I needed.

With the nun listening in, I told God everything. I told him what a disappointment I was to my mother, what a sorry friend I'd been to Danny, what a failure I was at everything I did—from ironing to getting pregnant to getting an abortion to losing my little Polly. My body racked with sobs, I felt myself pulled into the loving embrace of this kind old woman. She held me firmly while I let it all out.

Then, tears streaming from her eyes, she wiped my face with her handkerchief and said, "There now. Let's get you a drink of water."

She led me to a tiny room off to the side of the church where there was a sink. Drawing two glasses of water, she set them down on a chrome table and motioned for us to sit. I took two or three gulps of water, caught my breath, and looked vacantly at her.

"Mariah," she said, placing her glass on the table. "You've told God some very hurtful things from your life. I was privileged to listen in to your conversation. That makes me part of your problem and I hope to be part of your solution—if you'll let me, dear girl. We need to pray for guidance. He will know what to do."

"I don't even know your name," I said, looking at this angel of mercy, my lifeline to hope.

"My name is Sister Elizabeth Marie. If it's easier, just call me Sister."

"Sister," I said. "I want to know what to do. I have no one to talk to—other than Polly—and, as you know, Polly's dead."

She frowned. "God will always talk to you: you'll always find him ready to listen. And I will be here for you."

"Then tell him I need to know how to go on living."

"Tell him yourself, child. He wants to talk to you directly."

I don't remember exactly what I said. But I did ask God to help me through the pain of each day. I told him I wanted to be a good daughter and to honor my mother even if she never loved me. I asked him to be my Friend and to teach me how to be a good friend back to him and Sister Elizabeth Marie. I cried a lot and felt her soft hands on my shoulders.

When I was done talking to God, she asked me, "Do you feel better now, Mariah? Did God answer you in your heart?"

"I think he's going to help me."

"Did he say how he's going to help you?" she asked, as one who really wanted to know.

"Not in so many words, Sister." I thought she looked disappointed. "But I feel stronger now. Can I come back to see you and pray with you again?"

Her voice soft and low, she said, "Anytime. But there's another who can help you more—Jesus, God's Son. That's him hanging on the cross above the sink."

I looked at the pale figure hanging there. He had nails in his hands and feet and there was an open wound in his side. His face was contorted in pain. I turned to Sister Elizabeth Marie. "What did he do that he should end up like that?"

"Nothing, dear," she said, lowering her eyes, her head moving slowly side to side. "He did nothing wrong. He's hanging there in our place—he paid the price for the things we do wrong.

"And because of him, we can talk to God, just like you did today. He's the One who opens the prayer door for us to go in. He'll always hold the prayer door open for you if you ask him to. In the Good Book we're told that, because of Jesus, we can come boldly before the throne of grace and find help in our times of need."

"Then I'll always bring Jesus when I come to talk with God."

"Yes, yes, Mariah. That's the answer. Take Jesus with you wherever you go, and you'll never be alone. God will always listen to you." She turned to the cross and bowed her head reverently before walking to the door. "Dear girl, go home now and see how God answers your prayers."

"May I come visit you again?"

"Yes, of course. Come to the same side door. If it's locked, ring the bell behind this bush." She pulled a branch back, revealing a small doorbell. "There, you see? Ring it, and I will come."

Over the next few years, Sister Elizabeth Marie became the hands and feet of God. I don't know what I would have done without her because life hasn't been easy for me.

When my heart ached for Polly, we'd ask God to reveal something encouraging about her. Soon I could almost see Polly playing in the streets of heaven or sitting on Jesus' lap.

When I felt friendless, Sister would remind me that my best friend, Jesus, would never leave or let me down. When I drew near to him, he drew near to me.

When my mother rejected me, Sister and I would pray for comfort, and soon I'd feel his loving embrace.

As for my mother, I realize things won't get better. I've committed a crime for which there's no remedy—I'm female. I know I should move out and get a place of my own but I can't afford it. These days you have to have first and last month's rent and a cleaning deposit. Even a modest apartment is beyond my reach right now.

"Could you find a roommate to help with the costs?" Annie said.

"Getting a roommate would help but, honestly, for me the best part of moving out is being alone, enjoying total peace and quiet . . . no one accusing me or yelling at me for doing this or that.

"I'd thought about joining Sister Elizabeth Marie at the convent, but that didn't last very long. I don't feel holy enough to be a nun. Besides, I don't know if I'm cut out to be celibate all my life.

"As for men," Mariah said, patting her cheeks. "I haven't been very successful. I'm always so gloomy I don't attract many men in the first place—and those I do attract are generally worse off than I am." She looked across the table at me. "Liz knows a little about my current boyfriend."

I sighed deeply, nodding. If Mariah heard, she ignored me and continued to tell her story.

• • • • •

Rick began coming around right after Christmas two years ago. He says he was Santa's gift to me but he really thinks he's God's gift to the world. The first time I saw him, he was coming out of a bar over near the church. I had just left Sister and was walking home when he saw me.

"Don't I know you?" he asked. I could smell the beer on his breath at several feet.

"No, I don't think so," I said, picking up my pace. There was no place to go besides home, so I hurried on as fast as I could. He followed me.

A couple days later, he showed up at the house. I wasn't home but my mother invited him in. For some strange reason, they hit it off and began an unusual friendship which I still don't understand. It seems they're brought together by a mutual desire to torture the life out of me. Every chance they get, they belittle, mock, and humiliate me. Once they took turns hitting me until I passed out.

• • • • •

"Stop!" Emma shouted. "Mariah, I can't take anymore of this. Move in with me! I'd be a good roommate. I wouldn't yell at you. It would be fun. You'd like it."

"Yes, Mariah. You've got to get out of there," Annie added. "You can't continue this way any longer, not a minute longer."

"Well, for goodness sake," I said without a thought of what Bill might say. "You just move right in with Bill and me. We have plenty of room." *Poor, dear Mariah! And here I'd been blaming Rick alone for the bruises. That miserable mother of hers, I could wring her neck . . . .*

Mariah stopped in her tracks, almost in shock, at the two offers from heaven that had just rained down on her. Shaking her head in disbelief, Mariah looked like a child who had just found a wad of cash but wasn't sure if it was real, or only play money.

"Do you mean it? Are you serious?" She looked at Emma and then at me.

"Of course," said Emma.

"Dead serious," I said. *I hope Bill doesn't kill me.*

"I don't know what to say. I need to talk to Sister—to pray for God's guidance. I just can't believe it. You both are offering me a home? This is a true miracle—God has heard my prayer."

Mariah fell to her knees in thanksgiving and we all joined her on the floor. Soon there was singing as we lifted our hearts together to the throne of grace.

What a Friend we have in Jesus, all our sins and griefs to bear!
What a privilege to carry everything to God in prayer.
O what peace we often forfeit, O what needless pain we bear,
All because we do not carry everything to God in prayer.

Are we weak and heavy-laden, cumbered with a load of care?
Precious Savior, still our refuge. Take it to the Lord in prayer.

Do thy friends despise, forsake thee? Take it to the Lord in prayer;
In his arms he'll take and shield thee. Thou wilt find a solace there.

It was one of the most spiritual moments I've ever encountered in my many years as a believer in Jesus Christ. I will never be the same. *And I sure hope Bill will understand what I have just done.*

No one wanted this evening to come to a close—but of course it had to end. As we were putting on our coats and getting ready to brave the elements, Annie spoke up, "I have one last thing to share with you before this amazing evening is over."

With that, she opened a small bag of individual lace packets, each of which held a tiny sterling silver charm revealing one hand grasping another's wrist in a sign of victory.

"I bought these as a reminder to support one another and uphold one another. What we've just witnessed shows that we don't need any reminders to do that. We are one in the Spirit. Praise God."

Chapter Nine

Liz's Lost Boy

On Friday morning, Emma called, breathlessly informing me that she couldn't wait until Wednesday to get started on Mariah's makeover. She wondered if Carly and I would mind her spending time with Mariah over the weekend. She would work on her hair and nails and take her to a resale store near the apartment for a classy new outfit. "Mariah can surely afford $25, and anything over that, I'll kick in."

I told her that sounded wonderful! Smiling, I hung up the phone, trying to imagine the two of them picking out clothes together. Emma would skim the racks, looking for just the right colors, the right styles for Mariah. Mariah, on the other hand, would cautiously finger price tags, concerned for the cost, fearing the bill might exceed $25.

Emma would be all fun—humming, smiling, laughing, having the time of her life. Mariah would be all eyes—watching, wondering, wishing she could be more like Emma. *Maybe one day when her fears subside, Mariah will find herself—the person*

God made her to be before she was buried under heaps of abuse and criticism.

Then I pictured Emma sitting down at the kitchen table in her beautiful Tuscan apartment and showing Mariah how to fix her nails and style her hair. Knowing Emma, she wouldn't stop there—makeup would be next.

I could visualize Mariah looking around the apartment, thinking how amazing it would be to live in such a lovely home with a friend, her first real friend besides Sister Elizabeth Marie.

Feeling a pang of regret, I pushed aside my own desires to make a home for her. I had been thinking that what she needed was me. She needed a mother figure to teach her about self-respect and positive interpersonal relationships. Perhaps even more than me, she needed Bill—a father figure to show her how a husband should treat his wife. Mariah needed to get away from the Ricks of the world. "Santa's gift" was not good enough for her.

Yet, who could deny her the pleasure of enjoying her youth with another young person? If anyone could introduce our cautious Mariah to the thrills of spontaneity, it would be our youthful, impulsive Emma. *Bill and I can tend to be stodgy.*

Ah, well, how did that song go? "Que sera, sera!" Whatever will be, will be.

• • • • •

Emma couldn't wait to call me on Sunday. She and Mariah had spent all day Saturday together, shopping and styling. "We had an incredible time, Lizzie. You wouldn't have believed Mariah. She was like a butterfly emerging from a dark, old cocoon, flitting from rack to rack."

"Did you buy anything?" I asked, fingering the telephone cord.

"We found the most beautiful blue dress that accentuates her eyes, shoes to match, and a bag to die for."

I smiled, picturing Mariah the center of such devoted attention. "Did she have enough money?" *I can always help with that,* I thought.

"No problem!" Emma took a sip of something. "Then we went home and I taught her how to pile her hair on top of her head. I made her spend the night so she could practice on her hair some more." Emma giggled. "She had a bit of trouble at first, but I think she's finally getting it."

"Is she still there?" The telephone cord had become a twisted mess.

"No. She left a few minutes ago. I wish I could have gone home with her to run interference with her mother. She wasn't sure what kind of reception her new looks would bring."

"Does she need me?" I asked. "I could meet her there."

"No, she'll be fine," Emma said. "Oh, Lizzie, you won't believe your eyes when you see her."

"Maybe she'll drop by and show me on her way home."

"No. I made her promise not to come to Over Coffee before our meeting. I want you to be surprised along with everyone else."

"Oh," I said, disappointed.

"We're going to meet an hour before group on Wednesday to do any needed touch-ups: she's going to knock everyone off their chairs. This is the most fun I've had in ages."

"I can't wait to see her!" I said. "Does Carly know?"

"Not yet. I'll call her when we hang up."

"Emma, you're an angel to do this for Mariah," I said before cautiously bringing up the subject of Mariah's future living arrangements. "Did the two of you talk about rooming together?"

"Yes. I could tell she really liked the apartment and we got along great." Emma paused, and I heard the whistle of a tea kettle being removed from the heat. "I think she'll move in with me, but she wants to pray with Sister Elizabeth Marie about it some more."

"How would you feel about having a roommate?"

There was a short pause. "I've enjoyed my privacy—a lot. However, Mariah is so special and she needs me right now. So I don't mind giving up my space for awhile. Oops, there's the doorbell."

"You go answer. I'll see you at group—both of you!"

• • • • •

By the time Wednesday rolled around, I'd worked myself into a state over what I was going to share with the group. They knew the basics from my earlier "presentation," but I'd never really gotten into what Paul Harvey calls "the rest of the story."

I wouldn't be telling it at all except for the promise I made to the others last week. It had seemed important to them that I tell about my own painful experience since they'd told about their abortions.

I guess I can understand their feelings. Hearing their stories had been good for me. I'd had no idea how deeply the pain of abortion could penetrate the hearts of women. Thinking back over the weeks we've spent together, I realize just how far these women have come toward healing.

The first week they could barely take their eyes off their shoe tops. Their lips quivered, their hands shook. Over time, they realized that they were among fellow-sufferers, comrades, friends, sisters. Cautiously opening their closed hearts, they let the fresh air of understanding and forgiveness waft in. Airing their most bitter deeds, thoughts, and feelings, they were able to breathe again, to smile and then to laugh. Finally they could look to the future with hope.

Not me. I began our sessions full of confidence and bravado—the consummate hostess. I wasn't expecting so much pain as I probed areas that had been repressed for decades. I still can't look to the future with hope. Will I ever forgive myself for failing as a parent?

• • • • •

When Annie and Susan arrived, Carly and I were already setting up. I had ordered special desserts from Helen Bernhard Bakery to go with our coffee. After all, as far as the others knew, this was Makeover Night!

"I wasn't sure what to bring," said Susan. "So I just threw some of my cosmetics and samples in a bag."

"I brought along some scarves and pins for accessorizing, just in case they're needed," added Annie, looking around. "Where are the young-uns? They're ten minutes late."

"I think they want to make a grand entrance," I said, glancing at the door just as Emma breezed in—a modern-day Loretta Young.

"Ladies, may I present a new member of our group? She's a friend of Mariah's, even goes by the name Mariah. But as you will soon see, she doesn't look or act like Mariah. Ladies, our new member . . . ."

Emma stepped aside to reveal a tall figure dressed in blue standing in the doorway.

"Mariah!" We gasped in unison, "Is that you?"

She came through the doorway, gave us a good look at her face, pirouetted, and curtsied before breaking out in the biggest grin you ever saw. "You see, it is definitely me."

Tears sprang to my eyes—she was a vision of beauty. Gone were the oversized jeans and plaid shirts! Gone were the sneakers! Gone was Plain Jane! There, in front of us, stood a young woman in a form-flattering blue dress, with matching blue pumps, carrying a fashionable faux-lizard skin bag. Her hair was piled on top of her head and, except for one delightful rhinestone barrette glistening just behind her left ear, there were no clips or combs or chopsticks visible anywhere.

"Mariah," Annie said, her eyes wide and sparkling. "You look perfect. I brought accessories, but you don't need a thing."

I kept looking at Mariah. Something else was different. What was it? Then it hit me! "What did you do with your glasses?"

Mariah smiled coyly and raised one eyebrow. "You like?"

"I love! But can you see anything?"

"Sure she can," Emma said. "She's near-sighted only. So we ditched those awful glasses and found her a darling pair of readers. Put them on, Mariah."

"Ah, yes." We all admired Mariah in her fashionable new readers.

"I brought makeup, but it looks like you've got that base covered, too," said Susan, giving Mariah the once-over. "Honey, you are drop dead gorgeous."

"That's what I keep telling her," Emma bubbled. "She was so easy to work with. We did all of this on Saturday for just $35.00. Can you believe it?"

"Emma took me to this wonderful resale place where we found designer clothes at thrift store prices. Now that I know about it, I can go back. The lady was nice and said she'd help me pick out other things that would suit my shape and lifestyle."

Susan took a napkin and reached for the desserts. "Not to be a wet blanket, Mariah, but I'm curious. Do these clothes fit your present lifestyle?"

"Who cares?" Annie said, hugging Mariah. "When you look like that, you can go anywhere."

"Just don't make the same mistakes I did," Susan warned. "In choosing your lifestyle, don't look only on external appearances." We all knew what she was saying—don't rely on looks.

"I won't, Susan. I'll always remember what you said, and I'll always strive to be 'respectable.' I know beauty is more than skin deep," Mariah faltered, her voice breaking, "because I've seen true beauty in all of you. You've shared your lives with me and have welcomed me as an equal into your group."

"Well, honestly, Mariah, you *are* an equal," I said. "Why would you think we're any better than you are?"

She shrugged her shoulders. "It's just the way I look at things."

"Well, we're going to have to work on that. The Bible says to love others as you love yourself. What we need to do is help you learn to love yourself, Mariah Martin. That's what we need to do." I looked around the group and saw four nodding heads.

Then Carly looked over at me and smiled. "Liz, it's your turn. Maybe we can help you learn to love yourself, too."

I nodded.

And so, at last, it was my turn. The old saying that you save the best till last was certainly not appropriate here. My story could never be termed "best." But it is my story, mine and Jeremy's. Perhaps telling it all the way through will help in some way.

Sensing Jeremy's blessing, I looked at the group, cleared my throat, and began at the beginning . . . .

• • • • •

You're all post-abortive. As you know, I'm not. My story has nothing to do with abortion, though the end result was the same, a dead baby.

Abortion wasn't even legal or readily available when I became pregnant with my second child. Besides, I wanted this baby. Boy or girl, it didn't matter, just so long as it was healthy. Bill and I had a two-year-old daughter named Jessica, and we believed that two children would make our family complete.

Having experienced one birth, we were almost cavalier about this one. I didn't take any special precautions with my health or my diet and it never occurred to us to pray for our child. We weren't believers or even churchgoers in those days.

The due date was three weeks off when I started into labor.

"This can't be," I told Bill. "Mom and Dad won't be home for two more weeks. They're still in Greece, and I haven't a clue how to reach them. They want to be here for the birth; they're supposed to watch Jessica."

Nevertheless, the contractions were coming regularly—thirty minutes apart. Jessica was safely deposited at her other grandma's house.

At first, the hospital considered sending me home, believing this to be a case of false labor pains. However, my water broke and there was no turning back.

"Babies come when they're ready," we laughed, not sensing any cause for concern. I'd brought my knitting and worked feverishly to complete the soft yellow blanket to wrap my newborn baby in.

At last it was time to be wheeled into the labor and delivery rooms. In those days, we didn't have private suites. In fact, husbands weren't allowed to be with their wives. Surveying the small sterile room, I smiled at an attending nurse. She smiled back.

A woman was screaming in an adjoining room. *Why can't they make her stop?* It was really unnerving! As my own contractions grew worse, my fuse grew shorter. *Why can't they shut her up?*

My nurse told me that the patient next door was young and terrified. They were doing their best to calm her but weren't having much success. I wasn't having much success either—quelling the fears rising within me.

This pregnancy, which had seemed so uneventful and smooth, began to morph into something ugly. Things weren't right. I began to feel profoundly afraid, tensing up so that even the spinal I'd been given earlier didn't offer relief.

Shaking uncontrollably, I heard more frantic screams and again wondered why they couldn't do something for that girl. Then I realized that the screams were coming from someone in my room—they were coming from me!

My doctor arrived, the same one who'd treated me since I was twelve, the one who'd delivered Jessica. "Here, now, what's this?" Dr. Gaylord crooned as he took my hand.

"I'm afraid." I started to cry.

"There's nothing to fear, Liz," he said. "You've been through this before. Jessica was an easy delivery, and there's no reason to think this will be any different."

"It just feels different," I said, looking into his eyes for comfort.

"Well, it's not," he said reassuringly. "Let's save your energy for the work we have ahead of us. All right?"

His presence calmed me. Embarrassed, I determined to settle down to business. Soon, the mood lightened; and the doctor and nurses cheerfully prepared to deliver another miracle.

• • • • •

"Push, Liz," Dr. Gaylord encouraged, his voice sounding strained. "Push again. I know you're tired, honey, but you have to keep trying."

The concern in his voice didn't escape me. Occasionally, I'd get a glimpse of the nurses' eyes. What was that look? Alarm? Fear?

At last, after so many tries, the baby was born.

Silence enveloped the room.

Then, instead of the expected loud wail from my baby, I heard a wee sound escaping his lungs.

Finally the doctor spoke, "You have a boy, Liz . . . but he has some problems. Let me get you stitched up, and then we'll talk about it."

Lying there, waiting for the doctor to finish, I felt hot tears streaming from the outside edges of my eyes. My mind raced. *What did he mean my baby has problems? Why didn't they let me see my baby? I want to hold him. Please, let me hold him.*

Later—after what seemed an eternity—someone wheeled me back to my room. Bill was there, seated, his face drained of color.

"What is it?" I asked.

He shook his head and shrugged. Then leaning down, he kissed my face. Our tears mingled.

When the doctor entered, his face was drawn and weary, his eyes moist.

"You have a son. But he's not healthy . . . he won't live out the day. He has mul-ti-ple (he stretched out the word multiple) birth defects, organs exposed, likely hydrocephalus."

Bill and I both gasped at once. "But how, why?"

"We don't know how and we don't know why. These things happen—rarely, but they do happen. In your baby's case, something must have gone wrong early in his development, and from that point, nothing progressed normally."

He took my hand. "Liz, Bill, before you ask, I want to advise you, as your doctor and your friend, not to see him. I am afraid you'll never get over the shock."

When we began to raise objections, he said, "There's nothing you can do for him; the nurses will keep him comfortable. He *will not* live out the day."

"But . . . ." I cried.

"Take a little time to think about it before you ask to see him. I have your best interests at heart. Believe me."

When he left, Bill and I wept, our hearts broken. *How could this have happened to us? Did we do something to bring it on?*

Were we too complacent about his birth? Were we being punished for not regarding life with greater respect? Do we have any history of birth defects in either of our families? Well, not in MINE. Well, not in MINE EITHER. Was our doctor right? Should we listen to him?

Of course, Bill, my protector, wanted to shield me from any more hurt. He was inclined to listen to the doctor—after all, doctors know about these things. Ultimately, we decided to follow our doctor's advice. We did not go to our son.

The doctor felt I needed to stay at least two or three days in the hospital. For some reason, he kept me in the maternity ward which was the cause of great anxiety for me. Outside my room, I'd hear other new mommies and daddies walking down to the nursery to view their babies through the glass. I'd hear nurses bringing babies to the moms for feedings—all the while knowing that my baby was not being held or cuddled by his mother. *What kind of a mother would not hold her baby?*

I cried and cried, and cried some more. Finally, one of the nurses took pity on me and arranged for me to be moved to another section of the hospital. *What kind of person runs from her own baby?*

I was released and fled the hospital, fled to hearth and home, fled to my bed. I saw no one other than Bill and Jessica, and I clung to them for life itself. *How can you be so self-absorbed when your baby is dying in the hospital?*

For by then, you see, it was obvious that our son Jeremy did not die that first day. He lived a second day, a third, fourth, fifth. Finally, by the end of the eighth day, I came to my senses. "Bill," I cried, "our baby is a fighter; he's fighting for his life. We need to be there. We need to help him! I want to hold my baby . . . ."

Bill agreed. He went to the phone, called the hospital, got the head nurse in the maternity ward, and told her that we were on our way.

But she answered in a soft voice, "I am so sorry, Mr. Smith, but your son just passed."

We were too late. Jeremy had waited over a week for us but we never came. *What kind of a mother would wait more than a week before going to her child?*

Months later we learned that during that excruciating week doctors had come from all over the area to look upon this little "specimen." Because we weren't there to stop it, our child had become the object of a "freak" show of sorts—all very scientific, of course. *What kind of a mother would let this happen to her baby?*

An unfit mother, that's who.

It seemed people whispered around me for a very long time.

• • • • •

"Liz," Annie spoke gently. "What you did or didn't do hardly makes you an unfit mother. You were confused, young, in a state of shock. I don't know that I'd have done anything different than you did in those circumstances."

"I agree, Liz, with Annie *and* with Bill," Carly added. "I can't see that what you did makes you an unfit mother."

Emma's eyes registered confusion. "Why didn't the baby's birth defects show up in the ultrasound scans?"

"They didn't do ultrasounds in those days," I explained, glancing at Annie. "When we were pregnant, we didn't know till the baby popped out what the sex would be or even if the baby was healthy."

"Wow," Emma said, shaking her head. "No ultrasound. Hmmm."

I continued. "Nowadays, when ultrasound scans reveal birth defects, many surgeries can be performed in utero so that babies have a much better chance at a normal life."

"But there's a down side." Annie's voice was calm but her eyes reflected pain.

"A down side to ultrasound?" Emma said. "What?"

"Sometimes when ultrasounds reveal birth defects, parents terminate the pregnancy."

"Yes, that's true, unfortunately," I added.

"Would you have terminated the pregnancy, Liz, if you'd known in advance about your baby's problems?" Emma asked.

"I can't answer that, Emma. I don't know. I hadn't become a Christian yet and didn't have any concept of the sanctity of human life. What I might have done, or not done, is strictly hypothetical."

"How do you feel about it now?" Susan spoke softly, her hand resting lightly on her upper lip. "Knowing what you know now, would you recommend abortion to a woman who discovers she's carrying a baby with birth defects?"

"Never!" I answered, as emphatically as I could.

"You didn't have to think long about that answer," Susan said, looking at me somewhat puzzled. "A lot of people who are normally against abortion favor it in cases of fetal deformity."

"Are you one of those people, Susan?" I asked her, feeling a twinge of disappointment that someone who'd experienced the pain of abortion might still be looking for loopholes, loopholes that would kill more babies and harm more women.

She raised her hands, palms up. "Like you said earlier, Liz, I guess I haven't given it much thought. Until it happens to you or someone you love, it's all just theory."

"Since it *did* happen to me," I said, trying to keep my voice under control. "I have very strong feelings about this. I didn't fight for my child's life and I've suffered for what I see as a lapse of moral character for more than a quarter of a century. Though I couldn't answer Emma's question about what I might have done then, I know exactly what I would do about Jeremy today.

"I'd gather that little guy in my arms, and spend every waking minute with him. I'd see to it that he was comfortable and that his short life on earth was full of loving time spent with his mommy and daddy and sister Jessica. Then when he died, I'd be at peace, knowing we'd done all we could for this youngest member of our family."

Susan asked, "How often do people do that, I wonder?"

"Not very often," I said. "Like Annie said earlier, women are often urged to terminate the lives of their children because of some suspected disability. I've read that eighty to ninety percent of children diagnosed with Down syndrome are aborted."

"What!" shrieked Susan. "I don't believe that. Why would anyone abort a child with Down syndrome? They're the sweetest children in the world. There was a boy in Melissa's class. He was wonderful; everyone loved him."

"Yes, that's what everyone says. And children with Down syndrome can look forward to good productive lives—their life expectancy has risen from twenty-five to fifty-six years over the past few decades. They participate in sports, hold down regular jobs, and bring joy to those who know and love them."

"I can't imagine anyone terminating the life of a baby with Down syndrome," Susan said, shaking her head. "That's beyond belief."

"It's fear of the unknown."

"It's genocide," cried Susan. "It's wiping out an entire class of people."

"So, Susan, does this still seem like just theory to you?" I asked.

"This is my wake-up call, Liz. I had no idea."

I glanced over at Emma who was chewing her lip and seemed to be a million miles away. I could only guess what our little activist was thinking. "So, Emma, what's going on in that busy brain of yours?"

Emma straightened. "I was just wondering what could be done to help these families and their babies. Is it even possible to do what you wish you could have done for Jeremy?"

"Yes," I said. "There's something called perinatal hospice now."

"What's that?" Emma questioned.

"I don't know exactly what it is," I said. "But I heard about a program called Lavender Tree in the Seattle area. People say it helped them through a tough time, giving them the ability to focus on their baby's needs. When their baby died, they could move on, knowing they'd done what they could."

I drank some coffee and swallowed it with difficulty. "But, that wasn't available to us. And so we continued on our pathway to destruction, plagued by guilt."

• • • • •

Guilt often produces a need for penance, a payback of sorts. What on earth could I do to pay for neglecting my baby? I tried working for the March of Dimes, serving as an area leader for one of their fund-raising campaigns.

But that turned ugly when I visited Dr. Gaylord's office to pick up the donation. I was confident that his office would have filled all three of the coin cards I'd left. Yet when I went into the waiting room, there were no cards on display. *Did they fill them all?* My heart swelled with gratitude. Smiling, I greeted the receptionist.

"Hi, Sally. I came for the March of Dimes cards. Did you fill all three of them already? They're gone."

She looked away from me, an embarrassed expression on her face, and mumbled, "Dr. Gaylord said not to put them out. He said that if we sponsored one charity, we'd have to sponsor them all."

Feeling like I'd just been slapped in the face, I stammered, "Oh—well, where are the cards? I'll need to return them to the March of Dimes."

Unable to look at me, Sally said, "He threw them in the trash."

Speechless, I stumbled back to his office, opened his door, and just stood there with tears running down my face. I never set foot in that clinic again.

• • • • •

Feelings of depression flooded over me, and I began to obsess about death. If death could take my infant son, it could take my two-year-old daughter. By day I kept Jessica constantly in my sight. By night my feverish brain was tormented with nightmares of kidnapping or freakish accidents. How could I protect her?

The first order of business was to get her baptized. Why? I don't know. It was something to do—like purchasing an additional insurance policy. Someone had told me that Jeremy was in heaven, and I wanted to be sure that Jessica and he would be together if anything happened to her if I failed her like I'd failed him. *Unfit mother.*

The church that baptized her offered a preschool for toddlers. I enrolled Jessica and took her faithfully three mornings per week. Before long she began to ask me and Bill questions like: "Who is Jesus? Why did he die on a cross? Why were people mean to him?"

We didn't know. At that point in our lives, we didn't much care either. Where had Jesus been when we'd cried out for help, when we had prayed for someone "up there" to save Jeremy's life? He hadn't appeared too interested in us, so why should we be interested in him?

Of course, now I see things differently; but I was looking through a completely different set of glasses in those days—shattered ones, like my life. In today's culture someone would have advised me to get some professional help; however, that was "not done" back then. I wasn't crazy . . . merely wild with grief.

Instead I put on a Band-Aid. I compartmentalized Jeremy and the events surrounding his birth and death. That compartment was only opened on Memorial Day and his birthday, when we visited his grave. The rest of the time I moved on, placing one foot in front of the other, gaining speed with the passing years.

Occasionally and unannounced, the compartment would open on its own, eliciting a panic attack. Once I was in the grocery store picking out lettuce when a wave of guilt and remorse washed over me. Breathless, gasping for air, I ran from that place, leaving a cartload of groceries behind. Driving home, I nearly collided with a garbage truck. *Did I purposely veer into the truck's path, or did my tears blind me? What force kept us from colliding? Why was my life preserved when I hadn't lifted a finger to preserve Jeremy's life?*

People continued telling me that Jeremy was in heaven. How did they know? How could I be sure? And how could I be sure that I'd end up there as well? Was there any chance at all that I'd ever see my son?

As these questions dominated my waking hours, I began to rethink long-held ideas about life and death. Maybe my early childhood beliefs were right after all. Maybe there *was* a heaven and a hell. Was there a way to know? A rulebook with the plays? Maybe I'd better find out.

The bottom line? I found the "rulebook" was the Bible. The things I read there changed my life. I found security and hope in its pages and I put my hand in the hand of God-Man who gave his all for me even though I'd been spiteful to him. Jesus had a love that went beyond anything I'd ever known. I could entrust my life and my family to him.

Jeremy's journey on earth was brief, but he was safe, and I would see him again at the end of my own journey.

Over the next four years I made great progress. I received God's forgiveness, became involved in church activities, met wonderful people, found renewed hope. Yet, something was still missing—Jessica was now six and spent much of her time alone. She needed a playmate, a friend, a sister.

By then, it was no longer possible for us to conceive. Though the doctors had said the type of birth defects that Jeremy had were very rare, we feared a recurrence and had "taken measures."

We considered adoption and wondered if there was a child who needed us as much as we needed her. Discovering that few children were available in the United States, we contacted an international adoption agency. Within a year, we had completed the application process and were awaiting the arrival of our Korean daughter.

I want to make it clear that this child was not a "replacement" for Jeremy. If that were the case, we'd have adopted a son. We believed this child was God's answer to our prayer the minute we saw her picture—sad eyes, stooped shoulders, needy. *This child truly did need us as much as we needed her!*

We named her *Joy* in hopes that she would be able to find joy with us. Within a few weeks of her arrival, the sad little four-year-old with the downcast eyes began to brighten up. She'd jump and hop and make silly faces, racing her tricycle around the cul de sac, her new sunglasses doubling as goggles.

In the orphanage, the staple had been gruel, a watery porridge, which accounted for the fact that Joy was undernourished and undersized. From the day she arrived, Joy began to hoard food under her bed and occasionally I'd find her out in the garden munching on an ear of freshly-picked corn or a raw bean. On a regular diet of meat and potatoes, however, we quickly put flesh on Joy's bones and she grew a couple of inches. The hoarding stopped.

We began to move ahead with renewed speed and vigor. Our family was complete, two daughters here and one son in heaven with Jesus. Life was good, but not perfect. Whose is?

Joy had a stubborn streak a mile long and had a hard time accepting Bill and me as authority figures in her life. We were, after all, not her birth parents and she had survived without our help for three years in the orphanage, thank you very much. Though bonding was difficult for her, we continued to hope that she would connect with Jessica, for both their sakes.

But it never really happened, at least not that we could see. Although they were only three and a half years apart in age, it took several years for Joy to learn to speak English. By that time, the girls didn't have much in common. I guess they treated each other like many sisters do; but when they'd be sniping at each other, I'd hear the old voices. *Why can't you make them love each other? You really are an unfit mother. You're the kind of mother who wouldn't even try to save her own baby.*

By all outward appearances I was an excellent mother—my girls came first. I didn't work outside the home just so that I could be available when they needed me. When Joy began to have trouble in high school, both academically and socially, I taught her at home. There was never any thought of bailing out, giving up on this kid. *Well, maybe once . . . but it was a fleeting thought.*

Somehow we survived the teen years. Jessica graduated from college on a Friday and married her high school sweetheart on Saturday. Joy left our home at nineteen and married the man of her dreams.

The house suddenly became very quiet. With both girls gone, I needed something to do. Bill bought me this coffee shop to keep his "restless bride" occupied. That's when I began to discover that other people have problems, too.

The thing that I've noticed as we've gone through our stories is that when it comes to our children, we're especially vulnerable. Whether the issue is abortion, adoption, parenting difficult teenagers, it doesn't matter. We may not all have the same problems but women need one another. We learn from one another and encourage one another.

So that's my story. Thanks for listening. Pass the biscotti around. I'll get some hot coffee. *Whew, I'm glad that's over. I made it without breaking down!*

• • • • •

"Hold it. Wait a minute." It was Carly. "Don't anybody go anywhere yet." She turned to me. "Liz, I wasn't even sure you'd tell your story. But you did. And I'm proud of you. Yet, something's bothered me for a long time, and I think I just figured it out. May I share it with you?"

"Sure," I said. *Oh, boy, now what?*

"In front of the others?"

"Okaay." I gritted my teeth, waiting for the ax to fall. *What could Carly possibly have to say that I haven't already considered?*

She put her coffee cup down on the table and leaned forward on her elbows. "Over the months, I've tried to draw you out, to discover *why* you weren't enjoying the freedom from guilt that the rest of us are. You've confessed your shortcomings to God and have received his forgiveness. But you will not forgive yourself. That's been a mystery to me. I've prayed hard about it. Tonight I think I know what it is. I'm almost positive I have it."

"Well, tell me then, Carly." I took her hands. "More than anything, I want to be free of this guilt."

"I've watched you, Liz. You've heard our stories, how we all aborted our babies. We premeditated their deaths! Yet you've hugged each of us, loved each of us, and have held nothing against any of us."

"Why should I?" I said. "It's not my place to judge anyone. Besides, you're sorry."

"On the other hand, you carried your baby, your Jeremy, for over eight months, anticipating his birth, planning for it, loving him. When he was born, you were in shock, you were given bad advice. Your parents were out of the country and you had nowhere to turn. You and Bill were not believers, didn't have Jesus or the Bible as your guide. You made what you consider a bad choice in the circumstances, but you didn't premeditate any of it. True?"

"Yes," I answered quietly. "All of that is true." I took a sip of warm coffee to quell my mounting uneasiness.

"You can forgive us but not yourself."

I thought about it for a minute. What she said was right.

"It can only mean one thing," Carly said, her voice cracking. "You hold yourself to a higher standard than us."

Waiting for this to sink in, Carly paused. Then she continued. "And do you know what that is?"

I didn't answer. I needed time to process.

Again she asked, "Do you know what that is, Liz?"

"No," I said, shaking my head slowly. "What is it?"

"It's pride." She stood in front of me, speaking in a soft voice. "Liz, you can't find forgiveness because you've been confessing the wrong sin."

Looking me directly in the eyes, she said, "Liz, your sin isn't being an 'unfit mother.' Your sin is being prideful. Confess it, and see if you don't find freedom at last."

I slumped in my chair, feeling like I'd just been struck with a sledgehammer. Looking around the room, I saw stunned faces turn to Carly, then to one another, and then to me. No one spoke a word.

And then—I knew. She was right! I could see it now. If anyone else had done what I had done, I would have excused them, would have extended grace. But I held myself up to a higher standard than others . . . and what is that, if not pride? My pride had blocked the freedom God was extending to me all along.

I began to cry—great heaving sobs racked my entire body. And I laughed, raising my arms first to heaven and then out to Carly. We hugged and we wept. All my dear friends were crying too, because they understood that the burden had been lifted at last. It was gone.

Carly had spoken truth in love. And the truth had set me free.

The tears that spilled that night (and on through the week) were cleansing tears, washing away the accumulated residues of sorrow and bitterness and blame and remorse. At long last, I knew what it felt like to be *forgiven and set free.*

And that has made all the difference.

Chapter Ten

Continuing Friendships

Despite our best intentions, the group began to splinter. Susan was the first to drop out. Her life was busy, revolving around the children she loved so dearly. We encouraged Susan to spend as much time with them as she possibly could, even though it meant losing her. She keeps in touch, however, and reports that Corey is responding well to Jerry Edwards and is learning to control his anger. He and Melissa are gradually moving toward each other—and toward her.

Emma met "Mr. Right" and, obviously, wanted to spend every moment she could with him. She brought Mike by to meet us and, like a bunch of overprotective parents, we put him through his paces. Nevertheless, to Emma's delight, he received our unqualified approval. We all received wedding invitations last week and plan to attend together.

Annie befriended a homeless woman who visited the pregnancy center and she's trying to help Janice rebuild her life. Janice visited the group with Annie a time or two, but it just didn't click for her. Annie felt that Janice needed her full attention for the time being. We were sorry to see Annie go, of course, but encouraged her to follow her heart. She comes by weekly for coffee and keeps up on all the group members.

The pregnancy center asked Carly to start another H.E.A.R.T. group across town. Two nights a week away from Joe and the girls was, understandably, not going to work. Losing our fearless leader was hard. My heart will always hold Carly especially tight because she found the way to set me free from the guilt and shame that had plagued me for so long.

By the way, Carly and Joe found Eric and learned he'd been hospitalized for a short time after his meltdown with Carly. Because of his age, he was taken into state custody where he received counseling and therapy. Now, living in a group home, Eric is preparing to live on his own. It's been a long road, but he's well on his way to recovery. Carly has put the past behind her once and for all.

To my surprise and delight, Mariah came to live with me and Bill. She and Sister Elizabeth Marie felt God wanted her to spend time with a functioning family. I don't know how long she'll stay—I hope long enough to discover in herself a person of infinite worth and potential. Her mother and Rick have, for the most part, not been a problem. Her mother doesn't understand Mariah's newfound independence and Rick doesn't know how to deal with a strong man like Bill. Hopefully, someday soon he'll just disappear.

Mariah continues to work at the factory but is taking art classes. She's learning to paint and has dabbled in sculpture and pottery. She often writes poetry that reveals her gentle and tender spirit, a spirit that had been ridiculed and squelched all of her life.

I'm working on my own relationship with Joy, trying to build a new foundation on which we can form a loving friendship. Now that I've been healed of my own hurts, maybe I'll be more aware of hers. My great hope is that we as a family can forge strong bonds that will unite Jessica and Joy long after Bill and I are gone.

Occasionally Bill and I take weekend jaunts to the coast or the mountains, and Mariah fills in at Over Coffee. She makes great coffee drinks and specializes in the favorites of our dear friends who continue to visit regularly. For herself, Mariah no longer orders coffee-of-the-day, decaf "with room for cream" but makes whatever her heart desires.

Me, I still like my coffee black.

COFFEE SHOP FAVORITES

Biscotti Siciliani

(Liz got this recipe from a Sicilian family she spent a summer with in the sixties.)

200 grams milk
500 grams sugar
100 grams shortening
1 kilo flour
25 grams baking powder
3 eggs

Melt milk, sugar, and shortening. Stir. Cool for a little while in refrigerator. In another pan, mix flour and baking powder. Add eggs. Mix ingredients together and let sit for 3 or so hours. Then take spoonful of dough and roll it. Put in hot oven for about 5 minutes pressappoco (more or less).

Biscotti Italiani

(This recipe came from Liz's friend Sally.)

2 cups flour
¾ c. sugar
2 tsp. baking powder
2 eggs (room temperature)
1 tsp. vanilla
1 tsp. lemon extract
1 stick (4 oz.) butter
1 c. chopped or sliced almonds

Pre-heat oven to 350°. Combine the dry ingredients in bowl. Combine all other ingredients except nuts. Mix all together. Add nuts. Knead. Place on greased cookie sheet. Form into log 1" high by 4" wide. Bake 25 minutes. Cool 10 minutes, then slice on an angle. Place on side to toast, approximately 10 minutes. Turn to toast other side.

FAVORITE COFFEE RECIPES

Emma's Favorite Caramel Latte

("with skim milk, and extra caramel, please")

Double shot of espresso in a larger cup. Pour frothed and steamed skim milk down the side of the cup, causing the milk and espresso to swirl together. Add ¾ ounce of caramel syrup for every 4 ounces of latte.

Susan's Favorite Decaf Vanilla Latte

Double shot of decaf espresso in a larger cup. Pour frothed and steamed skim milk down the side of the cup (as in Emma's recipe). Add ¾ ounce vanilla syrup for every 4 ounces of latte.

Annie's Favorite—Cappuccino, lots of foam

Single shot of espresso. Add steamed milk and froth, heavy on the froth. Serve with these options: sugar, cinnamon, nutmeg, powdered chocolate.

Carly's Favorite—Double Almond Mocha

Double shot of espresso. Add one ounce of chocolate. Add frothed milk until the cup is almost full. Add ½ ounce almond syrup. Top with whipped cream and garnish with sprinkled cocoa.

Mariah's Favorite, coffee-of-the-day, decaf, with room for cream

Coffee of the day, decaffeinated. Do not fill cup. Leave room for Mariah to add cream.

Liz's Favorite, regular coffee, black

The shop owner, who could fix anything she wanted, preferred to drink regular French Roast, black.

Over Coffee Group Discussion Questions

Pour yourself and your friends a cup of coffee and consider each story. Ask what each woman might have done to improve the situation in which she found herself. Ask what you might have done in her shoes.

You may wish to dig a little deeper by researching the resources listed in the back of this book. Learn about organizations that are helping the hurting, and consider volunteering some of your time to make someone else's life better.

Consider starting a support group of your own on this or some other topic of interest to you and your friends. Telling one another our stories can be therapeutic in that it frees us from bondage and opens doors of communication to others. Be sure to follow certain guidelines to protect yourselves and your group. (A copy of possible guidelines is listed with the other resources.)

Discussion Questions (Carly)

Chapter 3:

1. What do you think accounted for Carly's interest in someone like Eric?

2. What would have been some appropriate actions for Carly to have taken where Eric was concerned?

   At the time?

   Later?

3. Why was Carly afraid to tell her parents (friends, church) about her pregnancy and subsequent abortion?

4. When Carly recognized that she, a Christian, was having suicidal thoughts, she was surprised. Why should Christians not consider themselves immune from such thoughts? On the other hand, what special defenses do Christians possess to help them through such temptations?

5. Some of the more common symptoms of post-abortion stress (PAS) include:
   Guilt, anxiety, difficulty relating to children, difficulty relating to men, depression, uncontrollable crying episodes, sleep and appetite disturbances, reduced motivation, thoughts of suicide, re-experiencing events related

to the abortion, preoccupation with becoming pregnant again, anxiety over fertility and childbearing issues, self-abuse/self-destructive behaviors, anniversary reactions.

Were you aware that there were so many symptoms associated with PAS? Why do you suppose many women have difficulty relating to men and children after an abortion?

6. In the United States 1,200,000 abortions are performed every year. According to the Alan Guttmacher Institute (the research arm of Planned Parenthood), approximately twenty percent of the women who obtain these abortions are evangelical Christian women. That means that every year ___________ Christian women obtain abortions. Over a thirty-year period, abortions could involve _________ Christian women. If even ten percent of them are suffering from PAS, that number would be ___________.

7. What message do post-abortive Christian women need to hear?

8. What ideas do you have for reaching them with truth?

9. What about the men who have been involved in abortion? Discuss who will reach them.

10. Carly talked about the Regional Memorial for the Unborn in Newberg, Oregon. Research whether or not there is one in your area. If so, consider visiting/supporting it. (Hint: In the resource list is the Web site for The National Memorial for the Unborn in Chattanooga, Tennessee. The National Memorial for the Unborn keeps a listing of Regional Memorials.)

    Why are these memorials important to families of aborted children? What value are they to the community-at-large?

Discussion Questions (Annie)

Chapter 4:

1. What is peer pressure?

2. What role did peer pressure play in Annie's immoral lifestyle in San Francisco?

3. Why do you think Annie returned to Rick for help even though she knew he did not have her best interests at heart?

4. Do you see a connection between the slogans of the sixties *(Look out for number one; make love, not war; if it feels good, do it; it's just a blob of tissue!)* and a devaluation of women and children, a devaluation of life? Higher rates of all kinds of abuse?

5. Annie was unable to conceive due to complications from her abortion. Do you see any connection between abortion and today's high rates of infertility? (For more information on this topic, you may want to visit post-abortion Web sites listed on the resource page in the back of this book.)

6. Do you see a connection between "free love" and today's high rates of sexually-transmitted disease?

7. Annie and other women her age see their work in pregnancy centers as a positive way of undoing some of the damage of the sexual revolution and radical feminism. What do you think about this?

8. If you know of someone who struggles with a past abortion and has never sought healing, write her initials here _______ and commit to pray for her. Look for opportunities to tell her about post-abortion stress (PAS) and direct her to a post-abortive support group, such as P.A.C.E. or H.E.A.R.T.

Discussion Questions (Emma)

Chapter 5:

1. Emma's generation has been saturated with cultural messages of evolution, sexuality, relativism, tolerance. Consider how these concepts can lead to confusion, especially in young people—whether or not they are committed to biblical standards.

2. How is Emma a reflection of her times, the post-modern culture? Who in your world sees things as Emma does?

3. Consider the different approaches for dealing with this confusion (education, political action, pregnancy centers, Silent No More campaigns). Try to discover pros and cons for each of them. Determine where, if at all, you see yourself fitting into a plan of action.

   Education
   Political Action
   Pregnancy Center Ministry
   Silent No More Campaigns

4. What do you see as the best approach for discussing these issues with young people who have been brought up with today's cultural messages (refer to question 1)?

5. What, if any, is the connection between today's confusion over sexuality and the epidemic of sexually-transmitted disease (STD)?

6. What do you know about STD? Consider the value of becoming informed about these diseases and how they are transmitted, especially as you have contact with young people.

Discussion Questions (Susan)

Chapter 6:

1. Like many women who have had abortions, Susan was a victim of sexual abuse as a child. Consider possible reasons for abortion to be common among survivors of childhood sexual abuse.

2. Susan had been abused by her uncle for years. The National Sexual Assault Hotline (see Resource List for contact information for this organization) reports that this is more common than we would want to believe. Why do you suppose these things happen? What can be done to stop it? Is abortion an acceptable solution in cases of incest and sexual abuse? Why or why not?

3. Why do you think that, from an early age, Susan had a distorted image of what "respectability" looks like? In the end, what did Susan finally choose as her standard for leading a respectable life? Discuss.

4. What did Susan mean when she said that she recognized she and Greg used each other to get ahead?

5. Discuss the dangers of playing favorites with your children. Who ends up losing?

6. Many of the problems Susan encountered (exhaustion, anxiety, living below poverty level) are commonplace in single-parent homes. Without becoming judgmental, what important lessons can we draw from this?

7. What help can churches give to families where there is just one parent in the home?

8. Discuss why or why not churches should take the lead in reaching out to hurting people and families.

Discussion Questions (Mariah)

Chapter 8:

1. Why was Mariah's mother so resentful of her daughter?

2. Mariah was an abused child. Other than the one teacher, we know of no one else who reported the abuse. Why is this not an uncommon situation? Discuss the reasons why people are afraid to report obvious child abuse.

3. A mandated reporter is one who, by virtue of her profession (teacher, nurse, counselor, etc.) is required by law to report child abuse. Consider the pros and cons of reporting child abuse even when you are not a mandated reporter.

4. At thirty-two years of age, Mariah wanted a place of her own. Yet she didn't think she could swing it on her income and was considering cohabitation. What reasons would you give her for *not* cohabiting with Rick?

5. What additional advice would you give her regarding Rick?

6. Mariah said that because of all the abuse she had suffered (including the abortion), she seemed to attract losers, men who dragged her down farther and farther. Why do

you think she made that statement? Do you think there could be some truth to it? Why or why not?

7. Mariah and her mother had obvious unresolved issues. Considering Mariah's age, what advice would you give her regarding her relationship with her mother? Considering the biblical injunction to "Honor your mother and your father," what boundaries can Mariah put in place and, at the same time, honor her mother?

8. How was Liz able to help Mariah without judging or manipulating her?

Discussion Questions (Liz)

Chapter 9:

1. What happened to Liz that had caused her such sorrow?

2. Has there been an event in your life you would like to "do over"? What part does forgiveness play in your ability to move on in life?

3. What did Liz discover was the reason she couldn't find peace no matter how hard she sought for it?

4. Has this ever been true of you? If so, consider:

   a. Have you left something undone?

   b. Are you confessing the wrong sin?

5. Discuss the viewpoint that only the perfect should be allowed to live. How does this line of thinking reflect evolutionary ideas, such as the survival of the fittest? In your discussion, consider Exo. 4:11; Psa. 139:13–16; Jer. 1:5; Eph. 1:3,4.

6. Concerning Liz's relationship with her daughter Joy, can you discern possible causes for their failure to bond? (Consider the possibility that Joy *did* feel like a "replacement child" or that she was somehow the cause of Liz's deep grief. Discuss possible other ideas.)

Carly's Resource List

Books

Randy Alcorn	Pro Life Answers to Pro Choice Arguments
Linda Cochrane	Forgiven and Set Free Healing a Father's Heart Path to Sexual Healing
Angie Cote	Secrets: A Healing Journey
Sydna Masse and Joan Phillips	Her Choice to Heal
Frederica Mathewes-Green	Real Choices
Meg Meeker, M.D.	Epidemic (How Teen Sex Is Killing Our Kids)
David C. Reardon	Making Abortion Rare Forbidden Grief Victims & Victors Aborted Women, Silent No More

Teri Reisser and Dr. Paul Reisser — A Solitary Sorrow

Thomas W. Strahan, Editor — Detrimental Effects of Abortion, An Annotated Bibliography with Commentary (3rd Edition)

Web sites

Abortion:

Elliot Institute. www.afterabortion.org
Eternal Perspectives Ministries. www.epm.org
Heritage House '76. www.abortionfacts.com
National Memorial for the Unborn. www.memorialfortheunborn.org
Priests for Life. www.priestsforlife.org
Ramah International. www.ramahinternational.org
Safe Haven Ministries. www.safehavenministries.com
Silent No More Awareness. www.silentnomoreawareness.org

Abstinence:

Abstinence Clearinghouse. www.abstinence.net

Abuse:

National Sexual Assault Hotline. www.rainn.org

Adoption:

Bethany Services. www.bethany.org
Holt International. www.holtintl.org
National Council for Adoption. www.ncfa-usa.org
CHASK www.chask.org

Ethics:

Council for Biotechnology Policy. www.biotechpolicy.org
Ethics & Medicine, An International Journal of Bioethics. www.ethicsandmedicine.com
Life Issues Institute. www.lifeissues.org

Polycarp Research Institute. www.polycarp.org
Wilberforce Forum. www.wilberforce.org

Feminism (Pro-Life):
Feminists for Life. www.feministsforlife.org

Medical Organizations/STD Information/Perinatal Hospice
AAPLOG www.aaplog.org
Centers for Disease Control. www.cdc.gov
Choices Medical Clinic (Perinatal Hospice).
www.choicesmc.org/pages/pregnant/perinatal.php
www.aaplog.org/perinatalhospice-infoforpatients.pdf
Christian Medical & Dental Associations. www.cmda.org
Medical Institute for Sexual Health. www.medicalinstitute.org

Pro-Family Organizations
Concerned Women for America. www.cwfa.org
Eagle Forum. www.eagleforum.org
Family Research Council. www.familyresearchcouncil.org
Focus on the Family. www.family.org
Parents Television Council. www.parentstv.org

Unplanned Pregnancies
Care Net. www.care-net.org
Heartbeat International. www.heartbeatinternational.org
National Institute of Family and Life Advocates. www.nifla.org
Option Line. www.optionline.org
Pregnancy Centers Online. www.pregnancycenters.org
Stand Up Girl. www.standupgirl.com
The Nurturing Network. www.nurturingnetwork.org

Guidelines for Small Study Support Groups

1. **Participation is the key to success.** Our desire is that everyone who wishes will get to share. Therefore, the leader will watch closely the time each person spends in sharing so everyone has the opportunity to participate. (Remember that in *Over Coffee,* the lengthy stories began once the actual support group had been completed.)

2. **Sharing is encouraged.** If an individual attempts to dominate or gets off the subject, the leader will bring attention back to the topic.

3. **Use "I" statements only in group discussions.** Advice-giving or "you should" messages stop the self-discovery process for both parties. Only share from your own personal experience of what worked for you when asked.

4. **No one is allowed to confess anyone else's faults but their own.** Our goal is to have an atmosphere of love,

acceptance, and forgiveness so people can feel safe to share their faults without judgment or condemnation.

5. **No sharing of specific abuse details.** Keep sharing of abuse histories in general terms rather than specific details, although you can share specific feelings.

6. **No one knows all the answers.** We are all learning together. It is not possible to come to a final solution at any one session. The purpose of the group process is to provide a safe place to express feelings, share, learn, and grow together.

7. **Follow Jesus' commandment.** "Love one another as I have loved you."

8. **Confidentiality.** What we say here stays here, except when you mention abuse of a minor, talk of suicide or of harming self or others.

Our group is a spiritual support group ONLY, not professional therapy.

About the Author

Julie Surface Johnson is an inspirational speaker and writer drawing from her personal and professional experiences to illustrate God's unfailing love. Her approach is story-telling, offering biblical solutions for problems women encounter in a friendly non-threatening way.

A known figure in the pregnancy center movement, Julie represented Care Net as their National Medical Services Consultant and, as such, enjoyed the privilege of working with leaders in other national and international organizations such as Heartbeat International, National Institute of Family and Life Advocates (NIFLA), and Focus on the Family.

Julie and her husband Dick live in Milwaukie, Oregon, and have been married for over 40 years. Their two married daughters and four grandchildren live nearby. The Johnsons have been active in Clackamas Bible Church for over 30 years where Dick has served as an elder and Julie is involved in women's ministries. Julie is currently at work on her next novel. For more information about Julie Surface Johnson and her books, visit www.johnsonsforlife.com.

Julie is available for speaking engagements and
can be contacted through her Web site
at www.johnsonsforlife.com.